OSPREY AIRCRAFT OF THE ACES • 6

Focke-Wulf Fw 190
Aces of the
Russian Front

To my friend Fritz
Merry Christmas 1990
Stephen J. Price

P.S.
Thank you so much for telling me
your story. History needs as many
gaps filled as possible.
S.P

SERIES EDITOR: TONY HOLMES

OSPREY AIRCRAFT OF THE ACES • 6

Focke-Wulf Fw 190 Aces of the Russian Front

John Weal

First published in Great Britain in Autumn 1995
by Osprey, an imprint of Reed Consumer Books Limited, Michelin House, 81
Fulham Road, London SW3 6RB
and Auckland, Melbourne, Singapore and Toronto

Reprinted Spring 1996

ISBN 1 85532 518 7

Edited by Tony Holmes
Design by TT Designs, Tony & Stuart Truscott

Cover Artwork by Iain Wyllie
Aircraft Profiles by John Weal
Aircraft Profiles Text by John Weal
Figure Artwork by Mike Chappell
Scale Drawings by Mark Styling

Printed in Hong Kong

ACKNOWLEDGEMENTS

Osprey duly acknowledge the assistance of *Herrn* Norbert Hannig and *Oberst
i.R.* Hermann Buchner, as well as the published works of Fritz Kreitl (*Tank
Busting in Russia*), Heinz J Nowarra (*The Focke-Wulf 190, A Famous German
Fighter*), Rudolf Nowotny (*Walter Nowotny – Tiger vom Wolchowstroj*), Alfred
Price (*Focke-Wulf 190 at War*) and Jay P Spencer (*Focke-Wulf Fw 190:
Workhorse of the Luftwaffe*) in the preparation of this manuscript.

EDITOR'S NOTE

To make this series as authoritative as possible, the editor would be interested in
hearing from any individual who may have relevant photographs,
documentation or first-hand experiences relating to the elite pilots, and their
aircraft, of the various theatres of war. Any material used will be fully credited to
its original source. Please write to: Tony Holmes, 1 Bradbourne Road,
Sevenoaks, Kent, TN13 3PZ

Front cover
**Having administered a mortal blow
to the engine of a 'snow-skimming' Il
2, Leutnant Walter Nowotny,
Staffelkapitan of 1./JG 54, presses
home an attack on a second
Stormovik over the snow-covered
plains near Krasnogvardeisk in
February 1943. A deadly weapon in
the hands of an *Experte* of the
calibre of Nowotny, the Fw 190A-4
made a telling impression on Soviet
aircrews during its first winter on the
Russian Front**
(Cover Painting by Iain Wyllie)

CONTENTS

CHAPTER ONE

'EXEUNT OMNES'

Tuesday, 8 May 1945. The last day of the war in Europe dawned fine and clear as the sun slowly rose over the central Baltic. There was no sign today of the low-lying, early morning sea and ground mist which had so bedevilled the Luftwaffe's opening strikes against Poland over this very area six long years before.

Flying north in the gathering light along the coastal sea lanes off the Courland Peninsula, the three-man crew of a solitary Soviet maritime-reconnaissance aircraft were confident that they would have little difficulty in locating and reporting the position of most, if not all, of the several large convoys (each composed of anything up to sixty minor naval units and small passenger vessels) which were known to be assembling off Libau and Windau. The presence of these ships in waters so far to the rear of the advancing Russian Army represented a desperate, last-ditch attempt to evacuate as many as possible of the tens of thousands of military personnel and civilian refugees still pouring into the last two peninsula harbour towns remaining in German hands. Once detected, it would be the job of the Red Banner Baltic Fleet's dive- and torpedo-bomber squadrons to ensure that few, if any, of the critically overcrowded vessels – and their human cargoes – should escape westwards to the safety of Kiel Bay and other such sanctuaries along the now British-held coastline of Schleswig-Holstein.

A 'new' Fw 190A-4 of II./JG 54 alongside a Bf 109G at Siverskaya early in 1943. The hinged fuselage fairing has been cranked back to allow the rugged up 'black men' access to the aircraft's twin 7.9 mm MG 17 machine guns sandwiched between the BMW engine and the cockpit. Despite having been at the frontline only a matter of weeks, the aircraft's whitewash finish is already severely weathered, particularly around the cowling and the exhaust pipes

The final view of Mother Russia for
many a Soviet aircrewman from late
1942 onwards included this ominous
head-on silhouette within it.
Fortunately for this photographer he
was sitting in a Luftwaffe aircraft
when he exposed this remarkable
shot in mid-1943

But so intent were the trio of Russians upon scanning the surface of the
sea beneath them, that they failed to spot a pair of miniscule black specks
off to starboard high in the eye of the rising sun. Within seconds the
hunters had become the hunted as the two small dots developed wings
and materialised into the unmistakable head-on silhouettes of radial-
engined fighters. The leading machine opened fire at maximum range.
Rather than diving away, the Russian pilot opted simply to increase
speed. It was to prove a fatal error. A second burst of cannon fire buried
itself in his right-hand engine. Only then did he seek the now dubious
protection of zero-altitude. At little more than six feet above the wave
tops, and with the observer and rear gunner hosing up a curtain of heavy
machine-gun fire, the dark green Petlyakov crabbed round towards the
safety of dry land. But the glitter of the single, sun-mirrored wake thrown
up by his one good engine betrayed the Russian's new heading as unerr-
ingly as any contrail. One more diving pass by the leading fighter hammered him into the sea. The Pe-2 disappeared in a sparkling flurry of
spray, taking with it Major Grigori Davidenko and observer Major
Grashchev – 'Heroes of the Soviet Union' both – together with their
anonymous gunner.

The two fighters, Fw 190A-8s of II./JG 54, resumed their westward
course for Kiel and British captivity. In shooting down the luckless
Petlyakov, they had not only both claimed the last of the nearly 9500 victories accredited to their parent *Geschwader*, as well as undoubtedly one
of the very last Luftwaffe kills of all of World War 2, they had also written
finis to the saga of the Focke-Wulf fighter on the Eastern Front, a saga
that had begun just 32 months earlier, almost to the day.

FAMILIARISATION

Originating in the autumn of 1937 with an order from the *Reichsluftfahrtministerium* (German Air Ministry) to Focke-Wulf's Bremen factory for a single-seat fighter to supplement the Messerschmitt Bf 109 then entering service, the Fw 190 was very nearly stillborn. There was a strong lobby within both the RLM and the Luftwaffe Operations Staff who argued that Willi Messerschmitt's superlative and world-beating 109 required no such back-up programme. In the event, and after submitting several alternative concepts utilising the liquid-cooled in-line powerplant then very much the vogue in Europe, it was not until Focke-Wulf's chief designer, Dipl-Ing Kurt Tank, began to argue in favour of a radical configuration built around a powerful 14-cylinder, air-cooled BMW radial engine that the future of the Fw 190 was assured. It is ironical that the only completely successful new fighter introduced on any scale by the Luftwaffe during the war owed its existence not to its own merits – classic though these turned out to be – but rather to fears on the part of the RLM's Technical Department that production and delivery schedules of the Bf 109's engine could be placed in jeopardy if it were also to be selected to power a second fighter!

The first Russian-based unit selected to re-equip with the Fw 190 was I./JG 51, the first wing of the 51st 'Mölders' Group. Blissfully ignorant of the contretemps surrounding the fighter's inception, the unit's pilots simply regarded their withdrawal for conversion onto the Fw 190 as a well-earned respite from the Russian Front, and a welcome opportunity, however brief, to return to the Homeland. Tracing its history back to

Chief mechanic Unteroffizier Rommer inspects 'his' Fw 190 which returned from ops to Siverskaya in mid-1943 with two complete cylinder heads shot away from its BMW engine by Soviet groundfire. Despite chronic damage to the powerplant itself, the pilot returned safely and made a perfectly routine 'three-point landing

I./JG 135 – a *Jagdgruppe* originally activated at Bad Aibling in Bavaria on 1 April 1937 – I./JG 51 had since participated in the invasions of France and the Low Countries, and in the Battle of Britain, before moving eastwards at the end of May 1941, along with the bulk of the Luftwaffe's striking power, in preparation for the invasion of the USSR. After two pilots, both of 2. *Staffel*, were posted missing in July, the *Gruppe's* third loss in-theatre had been that of the *Gruppenkommandeur*, Hauptmann Hermann-Friedrich Joppien, a 70- victory ace and holder of the Knight's Cross with Oak Leaves, who was killed on the Central Sector south-west of Moscow on 25 August 1941. Now, 12 months and three *Kommandeure* later, I./JG 51 was still on the Central Sector facing a new counter-offensive supported, for the first time, by the Lavochkin La-5 and the

Yakovlev Yak-7B, both of which were superior in performance to the *Gruppe's* tiring Bf 109Fs. It was at the height of this crisis that I./JG 51, under Hauptmann Heinrich Krafft, was pulled from the frontline and retired to Jesau, near Königsberg, for conversion onto the Fw 190A-3.

The conversion course itself comprised a series of technical lectures on the handling and flight characteristics of their new mount. The most obvious difference from the familiar form of the Bf 109 was the pugnacious size of the powerplant; on the Fw 190A-3 this being the 1700 hp BMW 801D-2. Ideally suited to the Eastern Front, the BMW possessed two important advantages over the Daimler-Benz: its very bulk offered a degree of head-on protection for the pilot, and it could absorb a tremendous amount of damage; qualities which were quickly appreciated in the low-level arena of the Russian Front where ground-fire was a constant hazard. Whereas the Bf 109 could be downed if nicked in the cooling system by a single rifle bullet, tales would soon be told of Fw 190s staggering back to base with one or more complete cylinder heads shot away.

One word of warning was sounded, however. If, for any reason, the Focke-Wulf's engine did stop, the advice was to get out – quickly. Powerless, the Fw 190 had 'the glide characteristics of a brick. As soon as the engine faltered, the nose pointed earthwards, followed by the rest of the airframe in close formation'. Opinions were to vary as to the advisability of tryng to land with a dead engine. Some pilots swear they never witnessed a single successful attempt at a deadstick landing. Others claim to have actually done so, with varying degrees of damage to self and aircraft. All are agreed, however, that such action was a course of last resort and not one to be recommended on a regular basis. Belly landings, on the other

'Like a bullfrog on water-skis' – two Fw 190s plough through the slush brought on by the spring thaw in early 1943. Devoid of any distinguishing *Staffel* or *Gruppe* markings, it is difficult to ascertain exactly who these Fw190A-4s belong to – if they are JG 51 machines then the photographs were taken at Orel, but if they hail from JG 54 then this site is probably Krasnogvardeisk. Note the mottled grey/white Fw 190 parked behind 'White 10' hand, offered the pilot a reasonable chance of walking away from the resultant mayhem. The forward momentum of the BMW, ensconced behind its armoured ring, tended to brush aside all but the most immovable of obstacles. The trick, one pilot discoverd, was in setting the prop blades to as fine a pitch as possible immediately prior to impact. As soon as they hit the ground, they bent backwards and doubled as makeshift skis. Some future ground-attack pilots would even profess to being able to make smoother wheels-up landings on their fuselage and wing weapons-racks than they ever did by perfroming a normal three-pointer!

The width of the undercarriage track also proved a distinct boon to Eastern Front flyers. Where the Bf 109 skittered perilously, the Fw 190 ploughed its way splay-legged and tail-down through the worst surfaces the Soviet winter could throw at it – snow, slush, rain or mud – 'like a bullfrog on water skis.' Taxying and take-off could, however, pose a problem. Despite the near all-round vision from the cockpit (there was a 15-degree blind spot immediately to the rear occasioned by the pilot's head armour), the obtrusive cowling precluded a full forward view until airborne. For unlike the Bf 109, the pilots were told, the Fw 190 had to take-off the same way as it landed: on all three points. Raise the tail too early and there was every danger that the propeller would dig in and flip the aircraft on to its back.

On the subject of flight characteristics, it was tacitly acknowledged that the Fw 190's performance did fall away at altitude. Although this was currently posing a problem on the Channel Front (and was to assume greater proportions in Defence of the Reich operations in the years to come), it played no part in Eastern Front operations where, experience had shown, the Soviets tended to swarm at low-level over the scene of any ground action 'like a plague of gnats at a picnic'. For the Russian Front, therefore, the Fw 190 was to prove the ideal machine, combining ruggedness with manoeuvrability and stability. In short a superb dogfighter – in all but the tightest of horizontal turns – and an excellent gun platform. The contemporary Bf 109 could only match the Fw 190A-3's formidable armament of two 7.9mm machine guns and quartet of 20mm cannon by bolting on two performance-sapping underwing gondolas.

The tactic evolved in the west of fighting the Fw 190 in the 'vertical plane' – in other words, a quick diving pass and rapid zoom recovery – rather than of mixing it on the horizontal, was also suited to the east where the enemy seldom sought the advantage of height and tended to pay scant regard to his rear. In fact, one of the Luftwaffe's major opponents on the Russian Front, the rugged Ilyushin Il-2 *Stormovik* ground-attack aircraft, was all but impervious to anything but a stern attack. While bullets bounced harmlessly off its thickly protected underside and flanks, a well placed burst of fire into the tail unit could often bring about its demise.

If, however, the pilots of I./JG 51 found themselves embroiled in a twist-and-turn dogfight, they were strongly warned of the Fw 190's one basic, and potentially lethal, flaw. In clean configuration the stall was sudden and vicious. Let the speed fall below 127 mph and, virtually without warning, the port wing would drop so violently that the Fw 190 all but turned on its back. Pull into a G-stall in a tight turn and it 'would flick over into opposite bank and you had an incipient spin on your hands'. But a virtue could be made even of this vice, Krafft's pilots were told. It was a manoeuvre no pursuer could emulate. 'Be prepared to control the spin, and it is one sure way of shaking Ivan off your tail. Just don't try it at low level, the initial movement eats up too much vertical airspace!' With this caveat ringing in their ears, the next stage of the course was cockpit familiarisation. There was, as yet, no dual-seat trainer variant of the Fw 190 available (a few appeared in 1944, but were used primarily to re-train ex-Ju 87 'drivers' for the ground-attack role), and it was crucial that each pilot be made conversant with his new 'office' before his first flight.

Pressing the button high on the fuselage side which released the retractable stirrup step buried aft of the port wing root, the pilot climbed aboard by means of a further spring-loaded handhold and step. Once in the semi-reclining seat, vertically adjustable over a range of some four inches, it was immediately apparent just how much of a quantum leap the Fw 190 represented over the Bf 109. The basic instrumentation could, of course, be recognised from old, but there was also an impressive array of new electric instruments and indicators, for the Fw 190 was equipped with a revolutionary and ingenious *Kommandogerät* – variously described as an 'early form of computer' or, more basically, a sort of 'brain box' – which relieved the pilot of such mundane tasks as the setting and controlling of the propeller pitch, mixture, boost and rpm. The Fw 190 was also a nest of electrics which, with the punch of a button, allowed the pilot to lower or retract the undercarriage (a separate electric motor for each gear leg), set the flaps and adjust trim. All this and more had to be explained, including the arming of the guns; first the fuselage machine guns and wingroot cannon had to be switched to live, then a three-second wait before arming the outer wing cannon – forget that delay in the heat of the moment, it was said, and you risked overloading the battery.

Finally, all was ready. One last check under the watchful gaze of the mechanic standing on the wing alongside the cockpit - shoulder straps, parachute harness, oxygen supply, run a not-yet-quite-practiced eye over the still unfamiliar banks of switches and buttons. The mechanic jumps down off the wing and takes station off to the left. 'All clear ahead?' 'All clear ahead.' 'Contact.' The BMW 801 is started by an inertia starter which is energised either by an acc trolley or the aircraft's own battery. A stab at the starter, and then the BMW roars into life in a cloud of blue smoke. Twelve degrees of flap at the touch of another button, release the brakes and start to roll. Unstick at 112 mph, punch the undercarriage and flap retraction buttons as, one by one, the pilots of I./JG 51 forsook theory and returned to their natural element. After a few cautious circuits and bumps, they were soon revelling in the superb control harmony of their new mounts, the lightness of the ailerons, the incredibly high rate of roll. Before long, they were practising dummy attacks on one another and staging mock dogfights during which they found themselves pulling aileron turns which would have wrenched the wings off their old Bf 109s.

The conversion course was at an end. It had been brief, but intensive. For Krafft's pilots – the majority of them products of the Luftwaffe's excellent and exhaustive pre- and early-wartime training programmes, and many already veterans of nearly three years of combat flying – there was neither the need, nor the time, to teach them anything more of combat tactics at this late stage. They knew exactly what they were returning to as they pointed their radial noses eastwards to resume the struggle.

JG 51 IN COMBAT

6 September 1942, the day I./JG 51 arrived back on the Russian Front, also marked the eve of the final German push on Stalingrad. Within 24 hours the strategically vital Gumrak airfield had been captured, German forces were probing into the outer suburbs of the city and Soviet Gen Andrei Yeremenko had withdrawn his battle headquarters to the far bank of the River Volga. Over the next four months the life, and ultimately death, struggles of von Paulus' 6th Army as they first attacked, and were then trapped by the resurgent Russians in the ruins of Stalingrad, were to overshadow all other events in the east.

Far from the battle unfolding to the south, I./JG 51 were initially assigned to the Northern Sector of the front, flying Fw 190-acclimatisation *Freie Jagd* (literally 'free-hunting') sweeps in *Schwarm* and *Rotte* strength out of Lyuban to the southeast of Leningrad. Within days, however, they were redeployed south of Lake Ilmen to provide air cover for the vulnerable bottleneck which supplied the Demyansk 'mushroom'.

In October, with the onset of winter, I./JG 51 moved south again, this time to the Rzhev-Vyazma salient on the Central Sector opposite Moscow. Like the Demyansk 'mushroom' 200 miles to the north, the Rzhev-Vyazma salient had also been created – albeit on a larger scale – by 'boulders of resistance' – bodies of German troops which had stood firm against the Russian counter-offensive the previous spring. It was to be here that the Fw 190's war on the Eastern Front would really begin.

Meanwhile, Hauptmann Grasser's II./JG 51 had retired to Jesau as the second unit to re-equip with the Fw 190. Their conversion was cut short, however, by news of the Allied landings in north-west Africa. As part of the Luftwaffe's response to this threat, 4. and 5./JG 51 immediately abandoned the Fw 190 and transferred to Wiener-Neustadt to collect 20 Bf 109G-2/trops, already resplendent in desert-tan camouflage, prior to staging south to Sicily and thence to the fighting fronts in Tunisia (see *Aircraft of the Aces 2 Bf 109 Aces of North Africa and the Mediterranean*).

To replace the departed *Staffeln* of II.*Gruppe*, Hauptmann Karl-Heinz Schnell's III./JG 51 were pulled out of the Rzhev-Vyazma salient to join the solitary 6.*Staffel* at Jesau for re-equipment with the Fw 190. This meant that I./JG 51 was the only *Jagdgruppe* defending the salient from within (although supported by the Bf 109s of IV./JG 51 based at nearby Vitebsk) as Soviet pressure mounted. No longer appearing in the huge, haphazard swarms which had so characterised the opening months of the Russian campaign, new Soviet aircraft – predominantly Petlyakov Pe-2 dive-bombers and the ubiquitous Il-2 *Stormoviks* – while attacking in equal, if not even greater numbers than before, were now operating in smaller, more disciplined formations. In the face of almost non-stop raids on the five major airfields within the salient – particularly the sprawling central complex at Dugino with its concrete runway nearly a mile in length, its hangars, barracks, supply and equipment depots – the pilots of I./JG 51 in their new Fw 190s were soon adding to the scores they had amassed while flying the Bf 109 (the *Geschwader* had achieved its 4000th

Dispersal on a frozen surface of Lake Ivan, west of Moscow, during the winter of 1942-43 for a detachment of Fw 190A-3s from I./JG 51. Note that the aircraft furthest from the camera is having its BMW engine changed background left. The *Gruppenstab* machines on the right clearly wear their distinctive chevron markings, as well as yellow theatre bands beneath the fuselage crosses. These aircraft were heavily involved at the time protecting Ju 87s 'dive bombing' supplies to the besieged defenders of Velikiye Luki

victory on 1 November). A newcomer to the *Gruppe* at this period, although not to the Eastern Front, was Hauptmann Heinz Lange. In fact, Lange had scored his first kill as long ago as October 1939 when an RAF Blenheim on a recce mission over Germany fell to the guns of his Bf 109E. For the past year *Staffelkapitän* of I./JG 54 on the Leningrad front, Lange had been appointed to the command of 3./JG 51 on 26 October:

'I first flew the Fw 190 on 8 November 1942 at Vyazma in the Soviet Union. I was absolutely thrilled. I flew every fighter version of it employed on the Eastern Front. Because of its smaller fuselage, visibility was somewhat better out of the Bf 109. I believe the Focke-Wulf was more manoeuvrable than the Messerschmitt – although the latter could make a tighter horizontal turn, if you mastered the Fw 190 you could pull a lot of Gs and do just about as well. In terms of control force and feel, the 109 was heavier on the stick. In the Fw 190 aerobatics were a pleasure!

'Structurally, it was distinctly superior to the Messerschmitt, especially in dives. The radial engine of the Fw 190A was also more resistant to enemy fire. Firepower, which varied with the particular series, was fairly even in all German fighters. The central cannon of the Messerschmitt was naturally more accurate, but that was really a meaningful advantage only in fighter-to-fighter combat. The 109's 30 mm cannon frequently jammed, especially in hard turns – I lost at least six kills this way.

'In the development of our fighter operations, the most significant step was our transition from the closed *Kette* of three planes to the four-plane "finger-fours" *Schwarm*. This innovation was developed during the Spanish Civil War with considerable help by Werner Mölders. I attribute to this tactic the high number of kills attained by German fighter pilots.'

Lange eventually became the sixth, and final, *Kommodore* of JG 51, ending the war with 70 kills, all but one of which he scored in the east.

On 24 November 1942, with winter really beginning to bite, the Russians pre-empted any plans for a renewed German attack on Moscow by hurling seven Armies, supported by a host of Frontal Aviation Regiments, against the northern flank of the Rzhev-Vyazma salient. The German central front was broken at Rzhev itself, at Byeli and at Velikiye Luki. The latter breach was the most dangerous. Velikiye Luki, a vital rail junction, had originally been captured by the Germans in August 1941 and since built up into the strongest hedgehog defence base on the Central Sector. It was now surrounded. As the only fighter presence in the area, JG 51's two *Gruppen* were hard pressed to answer all the calls now suddenly being made upon them – calls not only to drive off the Soviet air attacks being mounted with increasing ferocity all along the sector, but also to protect their own bombers attempting to drop supplies to the besieged defenders of Velikiye Luki. Thinly stretched though he was, Hauptmann Krafft was obliged to detach part of his I. *Gruppe* to operate from the frozen surface of Lake Ivan near to Velikiye Luki. From here they escorted Ju 87s 'dive-bombing' supply containers to the troops trapped in the hedgehog below. In December they were joined by III./JG 51 and by 6. *Staffel*, both newly arrived from Jesau and now flying the Fw 190A-4. But the Luftwaffe's efforts were to no avail. On 1 January, 1943 Velikiye Luki was stormed.

Meanwhile, along the northern flank of the Rzhev-Vyazma salient the main body of I./JG 51 had been suffering its first combat losses on the Fw 190. On 10 December Hauptmann Horst Riemann, who also served as the *Geschwader* Signals Officer, was killed in action. Then, four days later, Hauptmann Krafft and Unteroffizier Ritterbusch were both downed by *Flak*. Knight's Cross holder Heinrich 'Gaudi' Krafft, who had commanded I. *Gruppe* since May, and whose score stood at 78 kills, survived the crash, only to be beaten to death by Russian soldiers.

Unlike I./JG 51's earlier *Freie Jagd* sweeps, the pilots of III. *Gruppe* were allowed no time for 'breaking-in' their new mounts. Returning from Jesau, where the conversion had already cost them one casualty killed in a mid-air collison, they found themselves in the thick of the fray.

The pilots of JG 51 were hard put to counter the growing Soviet pressure which was being felt along the entire length of the Central Sector. There now began a period of 'fire brigade' actions as separate *Gruppen, Staffeln* – sometimes even individual *Schwärme* – were despatched back and forth along the front from one new area of danger to the next. By the end of the year I./JG 51 found themselves being rotated between Lake Ivan, Vyazma and Orel. Not unnaturally casualties began to climb, none more tragic than that of Hauptmann Rudolf Busch, who had taken over acting command of I. *Gruppe* after the loss of 'Gaudi' Krafft. On 17 January Busch took off from the frozen surface of Lake Ivan as wingman to *Geschwaderkommodore* Oberstleutnant Karl-Gottfried Nordmann. Still in a steep, climbing turn Nordmann must have let his speed drop away, for suddenly, without warning, his Fw 190 whipped over onto its opposite wing and smashed into Busch, who went down in flames behind enemy lines. The wounded Nordmann managed to parachute to safety, but the incident had so shattered him that, although he returned after recovery from his injuries to resume command of the *Geschwader*, never again did he fly operationally. During Nordmann's absence the *Geschwader* was led by Hauptmann Schnell, *Kommandeur* of III. *Gruppe*.

Early in 1943 III. *Gruppe* had been transferred to Orel. Here, on 29 January, Oberleutnant Günther Schack of 9./JG 51 had a field day. After escorting a formation of Ju 87s to their target, Schack's *Schwarm* were on their way back to base when they were informed by ground control that eight *Möbelwagen* ('furniture vans', the code for enemy bombers) had been reported crossing the German lines at Novosil. Closing up, the Fw 190s soon found eight Pe-2s flying in line astern. What followed was, in Schack's own words, a real 'turkey shoot'. Within five minutes all eight Pe-2s were burning on the ground, five of them claimed by Schack.

In the ten days following the destruction of the eight Pe-2's, III./JG 51 were in action every day. And by 11 February Schack's score had risen to 30. His particular forte was to attack and fire while turning, a manoeuvre that required considerable skill, and one which he demonstrated no better than on 23 February. By the end of that day I. and III. *Gruppen* between them had brought down a total of 46 aircraft. Five had fallen to Schack, three of them being LaGG-3s which he had shot out of a tight defensive circle of four in the space of less than a minute by once again using his favourite steep turn tactic – a manoeuvre, incidentally, which the legendary Werner Mölders had declared 'imposssible' two years earlier. By war's end Günther Schack would himself be a *Gruppenkommandeur* with 174 kills to his credit, all scored on the Eastern Front.

As February gave way to March, the crisis on the Central Sector was coming to a head. To the north the Demyansk 'mushroom' was slowly being cleared. To help cover the final stages of the withdrawal, III./JG 51 were deployed to Krasnogvardeisk for temporary assignment to JG 54.

In March, too, all hope of using the shrinking Rzhev-Vyazma salient as a launching pad for an attack on Moscow had to be finally abandoned. I. and IV./JG 51 supported the ground forces' withdrawal to the best of their limited ability, the former now being down to just eight serviceable Fw 190s, and IV. *Gruppe* little better off in terms of Bf 109s. After the salient had been collapsed and the frontline straightened, IV. *Gruppe* retired to convert to the Fw 190. In the meantime, I. *Gruppe*, now commanded by Major Erich Leie, were transferred southwards to Bryansk, where a new threat was developing. At Bryansk I./JG 51 again had the chance briefly to fly that one type of sortie most dear to the fighter pilot's heart – the *Freie Jagd*. And two new names began to emerge from the ranks of I. *Gruppe* – Joachim 'Achim' Brendel and Josef 'Pepi' Jennewein. Like 9. *Staffel's* Günther Schack, both were long-serving members of JG 51, but neither had particularly shone in the scoring stakes during their time on the Bf 109. Brendel's rise to fame was to begin in the spring of 1943. During the course of the next two years he would amass a total of 189 kills – all in the east – including 25 Yak-9s and, incredibly, 88 *Stormoviks*! Austrian 'Pepi' Jennewein, the 1940 world ski champion, had become an ace during the Battle of Britain. But it was not until he got the Fw 190 that he, too, began to show his talent, scoring as many as seven victories in a single day and, on one notable occasion, five bombers in just six minutes – instant 'acedom' doesn't come much quicker than that!

By the end of March 1943, however, both sides had flown and fought themselves to a near standstill. The onset of the spring thaw came as a welcome relief. Offensive activity was reduced to a minimum on the Central Sector as Germans and Russians alike sought to rebuild their strength for what was to be the next great test – the battle of Kursk.

JG 54 – ENTER THE 'GREEN HEARTS'

Back at the turn of the year, when JG 51 had been busy trying to bring succour to the defenders of Velikiye Luki while, at the same time, attempting to shore up the rest of the Central Sector, the second, and last, *Jagdgeschwader* on the Eastern Front to be re-equipped with the Fw 190 began conversion. The unit in question, JG 54 *Grünherz* – the famous 'Green Hearts' *Geschwader* – had not even been in existence as such at the beginning of the war having been formed from three hitherto disparate *Gruppen* only immediately prior to the Battle of Britain.

At the beginning of Operation *Barbarossa*, JG 54's three *Gruppen* of Bf 109Fs constituted the sole fighter strength of *Luftflotte* 1 on the Northern Sector of the front. Keeping pace with *Feldmarschall* Ritter von Leeb's *Heeresgruppe Nord*, the *Geschwader* marched swiftly through the Baltic States in the high summer of 1941, arriving at the gates of Leningrad by early September. On 5 September they occupied the airfield at Siverskaya, and that at Krasnogvardeisk (also known as Gatschina) a few days later. For the next year concentrated primarily around Leningrad, JG 54 was to lead, by Eastern Front standards, a relatively sedentary existence. Their zone of operations stretched from the Demyansk 'mushroom' in the south (where it co-joined with JG 51's left flank on the Central Sector) northwards to the shores of the Gulf of Finland and, sometimes, beyond into southern Finland itself – a front some 300 miles long.

In December 1942 the first members of Hauptmann Hans Philipp's I./JG 54 departed Krasnogvardeisk for East Prussia and re-equipment with the Fw 190A-4. This time, however, the destination was not Jesau, but Heiligenbeil, an ex-bomber station now serving as a major supply and repair base, on the main road and rail link some 30 miles to the south-west of Königsberg. Among their number were a duo who would rise to become the Eastern Front's most successful Fw 190 pilots – in fact, the fourth- and fifth-highest ranking aces of all times.

The first, an NCO pilot small in stature and quiet in demeanour, had yet to properly make his mark. Few would then have guessed that the hesitant, slow-spoken Sudeten-born Otto Kittel would ultimately be the *Grünherz-Geschwader*'s top scorer. During the early phases of *Barbarossa*, the 'happy time' for Bf 109 kills, it had taken Kittel some eight months to achieve just 15 victories. As with others before him, it seemed that conversion to the Fw 190 was to provide the spark. Where once the shooting-down of enemy aircraft had seemed to pose an insuperable problem, soon for Kittel there was to be no looking back.

The second future *Experte*, by contrast, already had more than 50 victories to his credit. *Staffelkapitän* of 1./JG 54 since 25 October, the career of 22-year-old Austrian Leutnant Walter Nowotny was almost over before it had begun. He had scored his first three kills on 19 July 1941 at the height of the *Geschwader*'s dash across the Baltic States, by despatching three Polikarpov I-153 biplanes over Ösel, the large island at the mouth of the Gulf of Riga. Hit by return fire from his third and final victim, Nowotny's options were stark: force-land behind enemy lines, or ditch in the sea. He chose the latter, setting the Bf 109 down off the southernmost tip of Ösel. Despite his care, he was thrown from the cockpit into the heavy swell. Inflating his life-jacket underwater, he was almost throttled by his parachute harness, which he had forgotten to release. Disentangling himself, he managed to climb into his dinghy. At last he could take breath, regretting only that his cigarettes had dissolved into a soggy mass and were unsmokable!

'Later I came to realise that it was a good thing I threw that packet of cigarettes away. I had nothing to eat or drink with me, and to smoke in the conditions I was about to face could have been my undoing. Luckily I had no idea of what lay before me. I would soon be found and fished out of the drink, I hoped, throwing my wet matches overboard one after the other to establish the strength and direction of the current and to set my course accordingly. So there I was, a little yellow dot on the surface as the sun sank slowly deeper and with no sign of rescue. I noticed that the current was carrying me southwestwards, away from Ösel. They'll find me, I thought, if not today then tomorrow. But just to be on the safe side, I wanted to to get as close as possible to the mainland which, by my reckoning, lay 40 miles away due south.

'So I began to paddle with my hands, noting with satisfaction that the distance between myself and the lighthouse still visible on the southern tip of Ösel was slowly increasing. Strangely, no notice had been taken of me by the keepers of the lighthouse; perhaps they thought I'd drown anyway. And then it got dark. It was a starry sky and I continued paddling southwards, the Pole Star at my back. Despite only having on a sports shirt, breeches and socks – I had kicked off my fur-lined flying boots while still in the water – I did not feel the cold because of my exertions.

'On the next day the lighthouse tower was only half its previous size. During the morning a number of Bf 109s flew past, but all attempts to attract their attention failed. Once, as two Bf 109s passed by quite close to my position, I let off a couple of rounds from my Mauser pistol. I also took off my shirt and waved it. But as it was dark blue, it didn't stand out very much. They didn't even spot the bright yellow dinghy!

'So I had to attempt the seemingly impossible on my own. This was a bitter realisation which didn't make that first day any easier. Later, it also became very hot and I couldn't quench my thirst. From time to time I held my shirt over my head to protect myself from the sun. But I needed my hands to paddle. By now the paddling motion over the sides of the dinghy had chafed the insides of my arms raw and they burned like fire, so I tried another method, throwing the small sheet anchor ahead of the dinghy and pulling myself towards it. At the same time I was having problems coping with the waves breaking over the sides.

Although this jolly looking fellow is not Walter Nowotny, the photograph does give some idea of the size of the one-man dinghy in which he spent nearly four days. This vital piece of equipment was stowed as part of the parachute pack, in place of a seat or back cushion, in much the same way as the RAF Fighter Command K Type dinghy of post-1942 fitted into a Spitfire or Typhoon

'There was nothing to be seen of Ösel anymore. I used my pilot's watch to set direction and course. The peace and quiet which I had found so restful after the ditching yesterday was beginning to have its effect on me; that and the water which was making me sore all over and threatening to fill the dinghy.

'The stillness of the second night was suddenly shattered around midnight as two black shadows approached me and, at the same time, fountains of water erupted a hair's breadth away. If they were Soviet warships shooting at me, I ought to have been able to see their muzzle flashes. From close up I recognised them as Soviet destroyers, steaming eastwards at full speed and coming under fire from the south. Frightened of being spotted, I draped everything I could find over the edges of the dinghy to hide its bright yellow colour. I remained undetected . . .

'Although exhausted by this encounter, it also gave me new heart. The fire could only have come from German coastal artillery. So the distance to the mainland could only be eight kilometres at the most.

'As the second day dawned I again saw nothing but water. The real battle with myself began; thirst, cramps and – above all – the pain from the raw wounds all over my body. "It's no good, you're a goner", I thought. Better finish it quickly. With my silver propelling pencil I began to write 'Dear Parents' on the edge of the dinghy. Perhaps the dinghy at least would be found.

'But as soon as I wrote the word "Dear", I threw the pencil into the bottom of the dinghy and tried to start paddling again. Twice I took out my pistol and released the safety, and then finally put it away.

A factory-fresh I./JG 54 Fw 190A-4 has its engine run up by its pilot prior to the first sortie of the day being flown from Krasnogvardeisk in early 1943. The gentle mottling of the winter white camouflage is clealy visible from this angle, as is the fact that the groundcrew have painted out the yellow theatre band that once surrounded the fuselage cross. Note also the carbon deposits from the starboard MG 151 20 mm cannon, which denote that this aircraft has very recently seen action

Lower engine inspection panels were often painted yellow for indentification purposes early on in the Fw 190's war in Russia – all three I./JG 54 A-4s in this shot exhibit such markings

'I awoke slowly on the third morning with a feeling of unease. A constant, cool damp breeze rippled over me. At first I could find no explanation. I drifted through a sort of cloud and, through the haze, saw a dark indistinct strip of coastline with spray being thrown up by the breakers crashing ashore. I paddled towards it, felt a gentle bump, was thrown sideways out of the dinghy and found myself on all fours on coarse sand. I pulled myself one or two metres up the beach – and then lost consciousness. Coming to, I crawled through a belt of barbed wire defences on the shoreline until I saw a farmhouse, and there must have fainted again.

Mission accomplished, a I./JG 54 A-4 approaches Krasnogvardeisk with its gear firmly locked down and flaps deployed. 'White 7' exhibits a full set of Eastern Front theatre markings typical of a newly-arrived JG 54 Fw 190 in the first weeks of 1943, including yellow wingtip flashes, fuselage band and cowling decoration – both yellow inspection panels and a *Gruppe* crest

'When I awoke, I was between sheets. My things were on a stool beside the bed, my pistol on top of them. To my horror I saw two soldiers in Russian uniform and lunged for the pistol. Just in time, I noticed their armbands. They were Latvian auxiliaries – the place was called Mikel-baka, a name I'll never forget.

'The coastal artillery men who looked after me were the ones who had fired at the destroyers during the night. They admitted to having seen something yellow in the far distance, but thought it was a buoy.

'Back at the *Staffel* (9./JG 54) they had already packed my belongings and were about to inform my parents. A week later, when I was back in the air, I got an unpleasant and oppressive feeling whenever I had to fly over the sea. It was not until a fortnight afterwards, when I sent a Russian bomber down over the very same spot near the lighthouse on the southern tip of Ösel, that I finally got over it.'

Although all this happened at the very beginning of his operational career, the events off Ösel played an integral part in Walter Nowotny's subsequent meteoric rise in JG 54. From that day on he never flew a mission without first climbing into his salt-stained, ripped and torn breeches. Nowotny's lucky *'Abschusshosen'* – his 'victory trousers' – became a watchword throughout the *Geschwader*!

Gradually the pilots of I. and II./JG 54 underwent a similar type of conversion course as had JG 51 before them. And, like JG 51, they too suffered at least one fatality; Leutnant Walter Beims of 3. *Staffel* losing his life when his Fw 190A-4 crashed at Heiligenbeil on 28 December. Nor were all members of the course as equally enamoured of their new mounts, one future *Experte* declaring disgustedly that the Focke-Wulf 'landed like a wet sack' and thereafter referring to it disparagingly as a 'wardrobe'.

Strangely, too, the instructional

Weak morning light in the depths of a Russian winter does little to warm this bleak view of a snow-covered flightline in January 1943. Every day the fresh snowfall was rolled flat by the diligent groundcrewmen prior to the first sorties being flown, with the excess being banked up as wind-breaks around the edges of the small dispersals

Seemingly oblivious to the roar of the BMW 801D-2 ticking over just feet away from them, two suitably insulated 'black men' turn their thoughts to Bavaria in July. The pilot, meanwhile, has gone 'head down' in the cockpit in order to check that the engine oil temperature is rising correctly. Once his dials indicate that the radial powerplant has 'warmed to the occasion', he will wave away both the trolley acc, parked behind the fighter, and the wheel chocks

The Russians had became more proficient at staging surprise hit and run raids on the Luftwaffe'e airfields by early 1943, and take offs and landings became times of great peril for Fw 190 pilots. Amongst the first things taught to new arrivals in the east was how to take-off from any position on the field, either from a standing start or taxying, and how to land quickly and safely from a low-level formation. Here, a pilot from I/JG 54 does just that, skimming in low over a huge snow bank

staff at Heiligenbeil appear not to have mentioned the Fw 190's propensity to flick over into a spin if turned too tightly. Certainly, the pilots can recall no such warning. Suggestions that this inherent vice of the A-3 had been cured by the introduction of the A-4 seem unlikely, as similar incidents were still being reported on even later variants during the final months of the war. The one feature of their new mount which seems to have impressed the young bloods of JG 54 most of all was its ruggedness of contruction, particularly the strength of the one-piece, through wing structure. This eventually led to an unofficial 'experiment' to find out just how much punishment the airframe could really take. Pushing his wallowing Focke-Wulf to its maximum ceiling, one of their number – who was, in fact, a veteran Lufthansa pilot old enough to know better! – then proceeded deliberately to point the nose straight down. The speed built up alarmingly. And although the sound barrier may have remained inviolate that day, such was the rate of descent that the propeller arc itself began to act as a brake. The pilot was no seven-stone weakling either, but it took all his strength to pull the complaining fighter out of its near terminal power dive and bring it safely down. The others crowded round to count the missing rivets, only to find every single one obstinately unpopped! As a confidence booster in a new aircraft, Kurt Tank himself could have staged no better demonstration.

Early in January, 1943, it had been decreed at a meeting of fighter commanders in Berlin that JG 26 *Schlageter* in the west should change places with JG 54 in the east. Fearing that a simultaneous transfer of both *Geschwader* would denude their respective fronts for too long a period, it was decided that the transition would be carried out piecemeal, one *Gruppe* at a time. In the event, only one *Gruppe* – plus one additional *Staffel* – of each *Geschwader* actually made the switch. This resulted in I./JG 26's temporarily operating for some four months on the Russian

Front – of which more later – before returning to the west in June 1943. For JG 54, however, it meant a complete parting of the ways with their III. *Gruppe*, which decamped westwards in February never to return.

Meanwhile, I. and II./JG 54's conversion was likewise progressing piecemeal. From January to March individual *Staffeln* gradually began returning to the snow-covered runways at Siverskaya and Krasnogvardeisk, where brand-new winter camouflaged Fw 190A-4s then shared hangar space and dispersals

with the less pristine Bf 109s (II. *Gruppe* would not relinquish its last Messerschmitts until August). Having been resident at these two large ex-Soviet bases for so long, the pilots had settled in to almost all the comforts of home. At Siverskaya, where the *Geschwader* HQ was fronted by two stuffed bears and large cut-out figures of Stalin, Roosevelt and Churchill stood outside the ops room, they enjoyed the pleasures of a cinema and sauna. Quarters at Krasnogvardeisk were even more luxurious, for tucked away in the woods alongside the broad runway was the one-time summer palace of the Czars, complete with ornamental lake.

Arguably of even greater importance, the groundcrews, or *Schwarze Männer* ('black men', so called because of the colour of their one-piece overalls), to whom every pilot owed an incalculable debt, were equally well catered for, with both bases having extensive hangarage and covered working areas. The only drawback was their proximity to the frontline, but the attentions of Soviet bombers and long-range artillery had come to be accepted as part of the daily routine.

Not all Russians were so overtly hostile, however. For the occupants of Siverskaya, which did not boast a paved runway, the advice of an obliging Soviet deserter on how to keep the base operational all year round was most welcome. After the first snow had fallen, he explained, half the field's area had to be rolled or stamped flat. This provided a firm, compressed surface for take-off and landing during the winter months. Meanwhile, the other half of the field was strictly off-limits. Come the spring, this untrodden snow quickly thawed and the grassy surface beneath was sufficiently dried out to permit operations from that half of the field long

Taxying in the Fw 190 was never straightforward, literally, as Hauptmann Heinz Lange of 3./JG 51 relates:

'When taxying, visibility forward was worse out of the Fw 190 than the Bf 109, but that was easily solved by S-turning. Visibility was also worse out of the Fw 190 during take-off and landing because these were performed in a tail-low attitude, unlike the Bf 109 which was fairly level at these times.' The pilot of this I./JG 54 A-4 has just opened the throttle to commence his take-off run down the freshly carved-out snow runway at Krasnogvaedeisk

The engine runs on the A-4 featured at the top of page 20 have obviously thrown up a snag as the pilot has now shut the BMW down and is consulting his 'black man'

Whilst the pilot secures the chin strap on his fur-lined helmet, his ever-faithful 'black man' frees his seat straps from behind his back – the ambient temperature can be gauged by the groundcrewman's ear muffs, which also serve the dual purpose of cutting down the engine noise once the pilot starts up the Fw 190's engine. The famous *Grünherz* emblem of JG 54 sits proudly below the cockpit

Rugged up against the bitter cold, a suitably attired member of I./JG 54 poses for the camera in front of an aircraft adorned with the *Gruppe's* distinctive Nuremburg coat of arms crest in January 1943. Quite who those booted legs laying over the wing belong to remains a mystery!

before the expanse of compacted snow used throughout the winter finally melted.

It was tricks such as this, and of keeping small fires going beneath the engines of aircraft standing in open dispersal pens to ease maintenance and starting, which made the harsh Russian winter almost bearable. During the worst of the weather most of the personnel at Siverskaya retired into the nearby village. Here they shared quarters with the local inhabitants, basking in the snug warmth of wood-burning stoves while the temperatures outside dropped to 40 degrees below, and only returning to their unheated barracks with the first signs of spring.

This cosy existence was soon to change, however, for coincident with their conversion to the Fw 190, JG 54 had reached a watershed in their history. The previous two-and-a-half years of hard campaigning, which had seen success in the air allied to huge advances on the ground, were over. The coming two and a half years, although they were to witness some local ground victories, and individual and unit scores' rising to unprecedented heights, would paint a very different picture. For despite numerous 'fire-brigade' actions from one end of the Eastern Front to the other, the underlying and irreversible movement would henceforth be one of retirement back towards the borders of the Reich.

The events of the early weeks of 1943 neatly encapsulated this reversal of fortune. On 13 January Russian fighters jumped a *Rotte* of 2./JG 54 east of Leningrad. One Fw 190 was shot down, but the other, piloted by Unteroffizier Helmut Brandt, force-landed on the ice along the edge of Lake Ladoga. Although Brandt managed to evade capture, his Fw 190 – black '2'– became the first to fall virtually intact into Soviet hands. On 26 January Oberleutnant Max Stotz, who had joined the Austrian air arm in 1935, scored his 150th kill with JG 54. On that same day the effervescent Major Hans 'Assi' Hahn, one of the *Jagdwaffe's* true 'characters', who had already achieved 68 victories in the west with JG 2 *Richthofen* before assuming command of II./JG 54 in November 1942, claimed his 100th victim. Then, on 19 February, JG 54 scored their 4000th kill of the war, as reported by war correspondent Scheuermann:

'In the course of the recent heavy air fighting a *Jagdgeschwader* on the Northern Sector of the Eastern Front under the command of Oberstleutnant Trautloft has achieved its 4000th aerial victory.

'Those taking part in the day's activity, which resulted in the destruction of 33 Bolshevik aircraft, included holder of the Knight's Cross with Oak Leaves and Swords Hauptmann Hans Philipp with his 168th and 169th victories, together with Oak Leaves holder Leutnant Stotz with his 158th and 159th, Oberleutnant Beisswenger with his 137th and Major Hahn with his 107th.'

Within days of this announcement, however, both 'Assi' Hahn and 'Beisser' Beisswenger were gone. A forced-landing due to engine failure behind enemy lines near Demyansk on 21 February was to cost the former seven years of Soviet captivity; – his final score stood at 108, plus another 36 unconfirmed. The latter, victor over 152 Soviet opponents was last seen going down over Lake Ilmen, propeller slowly windmilling, after being bounced by ten enemy fighters on 6 March. His fate remains unknown. Nor were the other two pilots mentioned by name in the above report to survive the year. On 17 March Hauptmann Hans Philipp became only the second Luftwaffe fighter pilot to reach the 200 victory mark. Promoted at the end of the month, he relinquished command of I./JG 54 to become *Geschwaderkommodore* of JG 1 in the west, where he was shot down by American P-47s in October. The fourth man, Max Stotz, would number among the high proportion of JG 54 formation leaders to fall victim to the blood-letting of the coming late summer.

There were other, unseen, enemies too, as one young Fähnrich found out to his cost. Norbert Hannig recalls the following incident:

'Early May 1943. I had some 20 missions under my belt as *Katschmarek* to an experienced old Oberfeldwebel (Warrant Officer), one Xaver Müller. On the ground he was a typically dour Swabian. But in the air, although cautious, he had lightning fast reflexes and always looked after his wingman. He already had over 40 victories to his credit, for which he had been awarded the German Cross in Gold (a decoration more commonly known among flyers as the "Fried Egg" because of its shape and size). I had been able to confirm a number of his kills and a mutual understanding had developed between us. I stuck to him like a leech, kept the enemy off his back and followed his every manoeuvre.

'That day the 5.*Staffel*, to which I was assigned, was at readiness at Siverskaya; the pilots dozing in the sun in deck-chairs, reading or playing endless hands of cards. Xaver was fast asleep next to me when the ops

At last, after an interminably long Russian winter, the first signs of spring thaw arrived at Orel (JG 51) and Krasnogvardeisk in late March 1943, and the whitewash was finally removed, almost – 'White 3' still shows large patches of winter finish, which contrast with the temperate green used elsewhere on the fuselage and wing surfaces. This odd mix proved ideal for blending a low flying Fw 190 in with the partially snow-covered terrain on the Eastern Front during the long spring thaw. Notice that the runway is still essentially compacted snow, which means that the temperature is still probably around freezing point. The cause of the smoke rising ominously in the background is unknown

This view of the same scene shown above reveals a fourth A-4 parked in the background receiving attention to its MG 17 guns

room clerk woke him with orders: "Herr Oberfeld (Chief), a mission for you. One *Rotte* to act as escort for a Bf 110 artillery observer spotting fall of shot for the railway guns at Mga. Target is the railway bridge at Schlüsselburg. The Bf 110 will be overhead at 10.30 hours and will fire a green flare to signal your start. You're flying black "2", Fähnrich Hannig black "12". The aircraft are ready. Your call signs are *Edelweiss* 1 and 2."

'Xaver nodded, blinked up into the sun, looked at his watch and said to me: "All clear? Another half an hour", and went back to sleep. It was ten o'clock.

'Fifteen minutes later we went to our aircraft. The mechanics helped us aboard and we strapped ourselves in. I looked across at Xaver and he gave me the signal to start up. A quick check of the controls before reaching for the starter. The engine coughed a couple of times and then burst into life. The groundcrew disconnected the acc trolley and gave the signal to taxy. I set the flaps to the take-off position and followed Xaver to the end of the grass runway. 10.27 hours. Another brief glance at the instruments – everything in order. I signalled this fact to Xaver and he nodded. We closed our canopies and searched the sky for the recce 110. I saw a small dot behind us and reported over the R/T:

"*Edelweiss* one from two, nightwatchman at 6 o'clock, *Hanni* (height) 1000, *Viktor* (roger)?"

"*Edelweiss* two from one, *Viktor, Viktor.*" Xaver confirmed.

'We got the green flare and took off as the 110 flew overhead. Formating ahead of it, Xaver waggled his wings to indicate we were assuming escort responsibility. We had no direct R/T contact with the recce machine. The weather was perfect. A clear blue sky, visibility more than 50km. The front-line lay along the River Neva which flowed south out of Lake Ladoga before turning west and emptying in the Baltic at Leningrad. The only rail link from the Russian hinterland to Leningrad at this time was the Neva. But every time the vital supply bridges were knocked out, the Russians immediately repaired them again. Now heavy 40 cm railway guns had been brought up to Mga, a village south of the Neva, to destroy the bridges at Schlüsselburg once and for all.

'The 110's job was to observe where the shells landed and correct the fire accordingly. To prevent the Russians from using their sound-locating equipment to pinpoint the position of our railway guns, a number of other heavy batteries in the area fired at the same time. From above the effect was like a giant firework display. A more active defence of the bridges was provided by the two Russian fighter fields at Schlüsselburg and Schum.

'We crossed the Neva at about 5000 metres. No sign of Flak. Below us was the railway bridge with the single track disappearing into the woods to the east. We could also clearly see the two airstrips.

"From *Anton* 1 to all cyclists: fighters at Schlüsselburg have been ordered to scramble, fighters at Schlüsselburg have been ordered to scramble." *Anton* 1 was the code-name of our wireless intercept station.

"From *Edelweiss* 1 to *Anton* 1, *Viktor, Viktor.*" Xaver calmly replied. Everything was going as expected.

'By now the first artillery shells were throwing up huge fountains of earth south of the bridge. Too short. Suddenly we spotted clouds of dust

Fähnrich Norbert Hannig poses for the camera in the cockpit of his A-4, 'Black 12', at Siverskaya in the early spring of 1943. Note his fur-collared sheepskin flying jacket, known as a 'Bulgarian' jacket because it was derived from sheepskin that originated in that country. Hannig finished the war flying Me 262s, with his score in the east standing at 34 kills

on one of the fields below – always two at a time, side by side. They were taking off in pairs, just like us. We counted up to 16. Four *Schwärme*, or 16 against 2.

"*Edelweiss* 1 from 2, 16 *Indianer* scrambled from Schlüsselburg."

"*Viktor*, close up – stick close."

'I positioned myself 50 metres behind Xaver's tail and continued to watch. The Russians were clearly visible as small dots against the bright northern horizon as they climbed in a swirling bunch towards us. By now the artillery had fired their third salvo. Detonations exploded around the bridge. The 110 dived away, its job done. The recce pilot waggled his wings to signal our services were no longer required. Now it was just us against the Russians. The dogfight could begin. "*Horrido!*"

'Xaver flew a wide turn to starboard above the group of enemy fighters. I followed tucked in on his right. We watched the milling mass of Ivans below us. One of their number started to loop. He loosed off a harmless string of pearls straight up into the air – no danger there. Another tried a clumsy sort of Immelmann which brought him up almost level with us 100 metres in front of our noses. A desparate break to port and he presented himself to Xaver as if on a plate. A short burst of fire tore the LaGG-3 apart.

I confirmed Xaver's success, "*Abschuss!*"

"Your turn, I'll cover you", he replied.

'I pulled ahead just as another Russian climbed up towards us. He fired and then attempted to dive back into the protective pack below. I looked through the Revi (gunsight). Range: 150 metres. My guns hammered. I could smell the cordite even through my oxygen mask. Streaming a long banner of black smoke Ivan dived away towards his base.

"He's still flying. Have another go", this from Xaver.

'I checked my tail. Xaver to the right, all clear to the left. Ahead and below me the Russian's smoke trail. I opened the throttle and followed him down, watching the range close through my Revi, 150, 100, 75 metres . . . now! I thumbed the gun button. My tracers buried themselves in their target. Large chunks flew off.

"*Abschuss!!!*"

'I was about to pull up when I was suddenly engulfed in a fireball. I was thrown against the right-hand side of the cockpit as the 190 went into an involuntary roll. Black oil covered the canopy – what the hell had gone wrong? I somehow managed to correct the roll and could just make out the horizon through the oil-smeared canopy. I levelled out, but then:

"Bale out!! You're on fire", Xaver yelled.

'My first thought: 15 kilometres behind enemy lines – that means Russian captivity. Immediate reaction: don't bale out until you have to. A quick check: no flames, so no fire in the cockpit. I tried the tap which sprayed fuel on to the windscreen to clear some of the oil. A distinct improvement. I was down to about 3000 metres. And now I could see the damage: my starboard wingroot cannon was split open back to the breech. There was a gaping hole a metre square in the wing. The right undercarriage leg was hanging down in the slipstream. The U-shaped oil cooler had been punctured and oil was streaming back along the fuselage. My oil pressure was dropping and the temperature climbing towards the red. But there was still a little time.

Below and bottom 'You can't teach a young dog new tricks either!' Hannig's dachshund 'Füchsle' ('Little foxy') flew no less than 20 combat missions sitting on his master's back parachute between him and the head armour. All attempts to teach 'Füchsle' to bark when he spotted *'Indianer'* on their tail sadly came to nothing!

"Xaver, get me back over our frontlines. I can still hold her", I said in clear, all thoughts of correct radio procedure forgotten.

"A bit more to your left and you'll hit Mga", was his reply.

'The Mga emergency strip was a small area in the middle of the forest, half meadow, half swamp, directly behind our forwardmost positions. Just three days ago Walter Heck, one of the 'old hares' of the *Gruppe* with more than 30 victories to his credit, had overturned trying to land at Mga. The armoured headrest had broken away and crushed his verterbra. He was completely paralysed and had died only yesterday. So, forced landing or bale out? First get back over our own lines. I turned towards Mga. Xaver was behind me.

"Watch out, Ivan's coming back again!"

'I looked up and saw a pair of LaGG-3s above me to port. They were positioning themselves for a copybook bounce. This could be it, I thought, as I turned into them and fired with everything I had. They broke away beneath me. Their canopies were open and I could clearly see their light blue overalls, tan flying helmets and the large, black-framed goggles through which they both stared straight at me as they dived past.

'I had lost even more height and was now down to 1500 metres as I again turned back toward the safety of our own front lines. I looked around for Xaver and spotted another machine closing in on my tail. I wrenched my willing black "12" into yet another 180-degree turn and opened fire.

"Don't shoot! It's me," Xaver's voice remained calm as he easily evaded my wild fusilade, thank God!

"Turn left, keep going."

'And there, only 500 metres in front of me, was the marshy patch of ground between tall banks of conifers. The landing gear was useless, and the flaps didn't respond. I lost height. The oil temperature was well into the red by now, the engine could seize at any moment. Ease off the throt-

Not quite an evening 'sing-song' around the camp fire – pilots from 5./JG 54 sit at a relaxed state of readiness between sorties amongst the trees at Siverskaya in May 1943. Amongst the group is ranking ace (173 kills) Leutnant Emil Lang (third from left). Due to an increasing number of surprise attacks by Russian Air Regiments all along the front, pilots rarely had time to rest during daylight hours by this stage in the conflict. Always on alert, 'Readiness plus 15 minutes' allowed the pilots out of their cockpits, but kept them at dispersal – as seen here – their aircraft allocated and ready. 'Readiness plus one hour' equalled aircraft and pilots on stand-by awaiting orders; 'Readiness plus two hours', groundcrews at aircraft, and pilots with free time on base; and 'Stand down until x hours', no readiness until the time indicated. The *Alarmrotten* were relieved every two hours in summer, and every hour or 30 minutes in winter. As soon as one pair was given the order to scramble, they were imme-diately replaced by the next two pilots on the duty roster

Two inseparable friends from II./JG 54, Feldwebel 'Bazi' ('Rascal') Sterr (left), who scored an estimated 127 kills, and Feldwebel Albin Wolf, who finished with 144 kills, seen on the Leningrad Front in May 1943. Both were later awarded the Knight's Cross before being killed in 1944 – Wolf in the east on 2 April and Sterr in the west on 26 November. The latter was flying with İV./JG 54 in Defence of the Reich duties when he was shot down by a P-51

tle, but the linkage had been damaged. Too much speed! Ignition off. The tips of the conifers were whipping past just below me at something like 300 kph. Landing speed was 150 kph! I tightened my straps. The prop windmilled. I couldn't get her down! The trees at the end of the strip loomed up at a frightening rate . . . I had to go round again . . . ignition on, she wouldn't catch . . . hit the primer pump . . . the engine howled and pulled me up just in time. Fortunately, I still had sufficient speed to risk one last, highly dangerous 180.

A second approach from the opposite direction, a sudden bang, and the propeller came to a standstill. The engine had finally given up the ghost. I quickly dropped the starboard wing and applied full left rudder, hoping the resulting slip would help to push the dangling right mainwheel at least part way back up into the wing before I belly landed. It worked. Planing across the watery surface, I eased the nose up. A few more bangs and crashes and I was safely down, skidding to a stop without nosing over.

'Everything was quiet – completely still. Unbuckle the harness and get out. But, like the throttle controls, the canopy release mechanism had also been damaged by flying splinters. It was stuck fast and I was trapped in the cockpit.

'Suddenly a hissing sound like a locomotive getting up steam. My first thought: "the fuel tank's going to go up". The second: "canopy emergency jettison!" That was jammed too, but I was able to get a foot behind the handle and force it downwards. In doing so I caught a hefty blow from the canopy side-frame as the release cartridge blew it off. But at least I was out, even if I was in the middle of a marsh. I saw steam rising from the hot engine as it lay in the water – that explained the hissing noise.

'I climbed on to the forward fuselage and waved up at Xaver who had continued to circle above me. He saw that I was safe and sound, waggled his wings and flew off in the direction of Siverskaya. Looking about me, I realised I was standing on the engine which was still attached to the cockpit section. Behind me the wings were sticking up out of the swamp grass with the undercarriage still attached. Further away still, right at the beginning of the long scar I had gouged in the boggy ground, lay the rest of the fuselage and the tail unit. All in all a good landing. The aircraft may have been reduced to wreckage, but at least I was able to walk away from it . . . once the airstrip's fire crew had rescued me from the swamp with ladders, that is.

'It turned out that the cause of the damage was sabotage. Somebody in the munitions factory – we never found out who, of course – had tampered with a centrifugally-fused explosive shell, which had resulted in its exploding in the barrel of my starboard wingroot cannon. The next round – an armour-piercing shell – then got stuck in the feed and was detonated by the following semi-AP round. It was pure luck that I was not injured. The cockpit, like the engine, had been sieved by splinters.

'While I was sitting in the sun trying to smoke a cigarette, a halftrack motor-cycle combination pulled up. Two army sergeant-majors, old sweats, each with a chestful of decorations, clambered off and smilingly saluted me, one asking, "Excuse me, perhaps you can help us. About 15 minutes ago a Focke must have come down somewhere near here. It was trailing a thick cloud of smoke. Up at the front we were blazing away like mad trying to keep the Ivans off its tail. Can you tell us whether the pilot survived?"

"Why do you want to know?" I countered.

'The other answered in a broad Bavarian dialect, "We've had a small wager. I say he made it. He", pointing to his companion, "bets me he didn't. There's a bottle of cognac riding on it."

"Congratulations", I said, "you've won. I'm the pilot and I've just about survived. That pile of junk over there in the swamp is all that's left of my Focke though." I was promptly invited back up to the forward trenches to help dispose of the winnings, but sadly I had to decline as I was expecting to be picked up by someone from Siverskaya.

'About an hour later a Klemm Kl-35, the *Geschwader*'s runabout, came in to land. It taxied up to the barracks where I was still sitting and Xaver climbed out. He held out his hand, "Congratulations! Well done, all of it. Wounded? Come on, the chief and all the others are waiting back at base."

'The following day I flew my next mission with Xaver. This time it was to escort a formation of Stukas – just routine.'

Norbert Hannig's luck was to hold. He survived the war, having achieved 34 victories with II./JG 54 in the east before converting on to Me 262s during the closing weeks. But Oberfeldwebel Xaver Müller, the quiet Swabian, was not so fortunate. He would be killed in action three months later, on 27 August 1943, his final score standing at 47 enemy aircraft destroyed.

Thus the spring ended with JG 54's two *Gruppen*, having lost some dozen pilots since the beginning of the year, stretched thinly along the length of their own front and beyond, southwards to the Rzhev-Vyazma salient and Orel, as they too awaited the Kursk offensive.

A bomb-carrying Fw 190 seen in the spring of 1943. The weapon mounted to the centreline ventral stores rack is an SB 500 kg High Explosive (HE) bomb. This type of weapon was the favoured ordnance for the *Gruppe* on the Russian Front, although a single SB 1000 kg bomb could also be carried, as well as smaller 250 and multiple 50 kg devices

This bombed-up Fw 190A-4 is a bit of a mystery machine as it wears both JG 54-type summer camouflage and a yellow theatre band behind the fuselage cross, but it has an individual letter instead of a number forward of the national insignia. This perhaps indicates that the aircraft belongs to the *Grünherz*'s semi-autonomous *Jabostaffel*. Note the *Rotte* of Bf 109Gs taking off behind the parked Fw 190

. . . AND OTHERS

While the four *Gruppen* of JGs 51 and 54 had provided the main Fw 190 presence on the Eastern Front during the early months of 1943, there had been two other *Jagdgeschwader* operating the Focke-Wulf against the Russians.

The first of these, as already mentioned, was JG 26 *Schlageter*, whose I. *Gruppe* had been ordered to exchange places with III./JG 54. In reality, only the pilots and certain key members of the *Gruppenstab* and ground-crews were to make the move from northern France, and that by rail; the majority of the mechanics and equipment were left behind to await the arrival of III./JG 54. The party, under *Gruppenkommandeur* Johannes Seifert, entrained for Heiligenbeil late in January 1943.

There they collected their factory-fresh Fw 190A-5s before staging via Riga to their destination Ryelbitzi. Situated west of Lake Ilmen, this was another of JG 54's bases of long standing, having also first been occupied back in September 1941. A typical *Feldflugplatz* (frontline airstrip), Ryel-bitzi did not boast all the facilities of a Krasnogvardeisk or Siverskaya, but accommodation in the thatched huts of the local village – if not exactly up to chateau standards – provided adequate protection against the elements. While the *Schwarze Männer* left at Ryelbitzi by the departed, Bf 109-equipped III./JG 54 familiarised themselves with the Fw 190, the pilots of I./JG 26 were briefed on their new area of operations. Eastern Front missions were perforce very different from those they were accustomed to in the west: low-level, small formations were the watchwords, keep a sharp eye open for Soviet Flak and, above all, try to maintain a sense of location and direction in relation to the German lines, however difficult this might at first appear when flying over a vast, unfamiliar and near featureless snowscape. Few who forced-landed behind the enemy's lines returned to tell the tale. Experienced pilots' preferred, whenever possible, to remain within safe gliding distance of friendly territory.

I./JG 26's first action in the east took place on 16 February when they downed 11 Il-2 *Stormoviks* without loss to themselves while helping to cover the ground forces' withdrawal from the Demyansk 'mushroom'. But this auspicious start was somewhat marred 24 hours later by their first casualties, when two NCO pilots apparently fell victim to their new surroundings. One was brought down by Flak, the other hit the ground while attempting to attack a formation of low-flying Il-2s. A third was fortunate to survive a crash-landing after being set upon by fighters.

The Demyansk 'mushroom' operations continued for the next month, by the end of which time the *Gruppe* had claimed 75 kills; 14 of them on 5 March alone, and with Hauptmann Walter Hoeckner, *Staffelkapitän* of 1./JG 26, downing four *Stormoviks* and two lend-lease Tomahawks in a single day.

With the staged collapse of the Demyansk 'mushroom' successfully completed, the *Gruppe* was transferred southwards in mid-March, via Dno, to Shatalovka near Smolensk. From here they operated in support of the final stages of the withdrawal from the larger Rzhev-Vyazma salient. Aerial activity was winding down, however, so much so that Hauptmann Rolf Hermichen's 3.*Staffel* was temporarily detached to Ossinovka during May for anti-partisan duties.

By now it was becoming clear to Generalmajor Adolf Galland, *Inspekteur der Jagdflieger* and leading light behind the whole exchange scheme, that the experiment was not proving a success. The folly of employing experienced Channel Front fighter-pilots – the first line of defence against the ever-increasing tenor of the RAF and USAF's incursions into western Europe – simply to chase partisans through the Russian boondocks was all too obvious. And early in June I./JG 26 vacated Orel-West to return to northern France. During their four-month sojourn on the Russian Front they had claimed 126 Soviet aircraft destroyed, of which 17 were, in fact, lend-lease American machines, including one oddity – a Curtiss O-52 Owl shot down while purportedly carrying out a Lysander-like partisan supply operation. Against this they had suffered the loss of nine of their own pilots. Among the returnees were a number of newly fledged *Fw 190 Aces of the Russian Front*, such as the aforementioned Walter Hoeckner, *Gruppenkommandeur* Johannes Seifert with 11 victories to his credit and 2.*Staffel*'s Feldwebel Karl 'Charlie' Willius with 9.

The departure of I.*Gruppe* was not quite the end of JG 26's Eastern Front foray. A single *Staffel* of each *Geschwader* had also exchanged places – 7./JG 26 with 4./JG 54. Hauptmann Klaus Mietusch's 7.*Staffel* arrived at Krasnogvardeisk late in February, where it was subordinated to I./JG 54. Remaining on the Leningrad Front throughout its entire stay in the east, 7./JG 26 had achieved some 63 victories before retiring back to France in July. The lion's share of the kills had gone to just three pilots: *Staffelkapitän* Mietusch, Oberfeldwebel Heinz Kemethmueller and Feldwebel Erich Jauer.

The fourth *Jagdgeschwader* to field the Focke-Wulf against the Soviets did so only in single *Staffel* strength, and then only along the very northernmost periphery of the front. After a lengthy and complicated period of gestation JG 5 - the *Eismeer*, or 'Arctic Ocean' *Geschwader* – had evolved into a microcosm of the Luftwaffe itself. Split down the middle, it was facing and fighting in two directions at once: against the Allies to the west, and the Russians in the east.

By 1943 I. and IV./JG 5, flying the Fw 190, were based along the Norwegian seaboard where they formed the right-hand flank of the continuous, if thinly stretched, arc of Luftwaffe fighter defences guarding the English Channel and North Sea coastlines from Ushant to Narvik. In the east the two Bf 109-equipped *Gruppen*, II. and III./JG 5, pitted themselves against the Soviets along the 850 mile length of the Finnish Front, from the Gulf of Finland in the south to Murmansk in the north. Apart from a brief deployment by IV./JG 5 to reinforce III.*Gruppe* in the early autumn of 1944 during the German withdrawal from Finland and northern Norway, JG 5's Fw 190s thus saw no service against the Soviet enemy.

In mid-February 1943, however, the *Geschwader* established a semi-autonomous fighter-bomber *Staffel*. Activated at Petsamo under Hauptmann Friedrich-Wilhelm Strakeljahn, the Fw 190A-2s and A-3s of 14.(*Jabo*)/JG 5 were tasked primarily with combating the Soviet coastal traffic plying along the Arctic Ocean seabord. This they proceeded to do with great success; the tonnage sunk, both of merchantmen and Soviet naval units, rising steadily in the coming months. One particular three-day period early in May, during which they claimed two 'M'-class submarines destroyed (by Feldwebel Froscheck and Unteroffizier Fohl) and a 2000-ton auxiliary and 3000-ton freighter (both by Strakeljahn), brought well-merited, teleprinted recognition from on high. From the C-in-C *Luftflotte* 5:

'To: 14.(*Jabo*)/JG 5 Petsamo   11.5.1943
For the excellent successes of the past days my very special appreciation.
                                        Generaloberst Stumpff.'

. . . and five days later:

'From *Fliegerführer Nord (Ost)*   16.5.1943
To: 14.(*Jabo*)/JG 5 Petsamo
Following teletype for attention of all personnel:
'The Führer has expressed his recognition of the attacks on shipping carried out by the *Jabos* of *Flg.Fü.Nord(Ost)*, and further conveys his wishes that these operations be continued with all available means.'

Although principally an anti-shipping unit (by the years's end tonnage sent to the bottom totalled some 39,000 BRT), 14.(*Jabo*)/JG 5 inevitably came into contact with defending Russian fighters, of which they also managed to take their toll. When awarded his Knight's Cross on 19 August for outstanding leadership, for example, 'Straks' Strakejahn already had nine kills to his credit. In April 1944 the unit was transferred from the Arctic to the sunnier climes of the Italian theatre, where it was redesignated and incorporated into the ground-attack arm as 4./SG 4.

Fw 190A-3 'Black 5' of 14.(*Jabo*)/JG 5, based at Petsamo, Finland, on the Arctic Front in early spring 1943. Led by Hauptmann Friedrich-Wilhelm Strakeljahn, this small *Staffel* wreaked havoc on the previously unmolested Soviet coastal traffic in the area – so much so that the outfit was personally congratulated by the Führer himself in May 1943. 'Straks' Strakeljahn himself also became an ace during this period, destroying nine Russian aircraft. This aircraft is painted up in standard early Fw 190 colours, and lacks the yellow theatre flashes. It does, however, boast the *Staffel*'s unique 'bow and bomb' badge on its engine cowl. Also, note the SC 250 (foreground) and 500 kg bombs sitting behind the clutch of 'black men'

ZITADELLE

On the major fighting fronts of the Northern, Central and, to a much lesser extent, Southern Sectors the full weight of the Fw 190 fighter presence in the Soviet Union continued to be felt (if 'full weight' be the proper term to describe a force whose numbers never once topped the 200 mark, and this along a front currently some 1200 miles in length!). In fact, the weeks prior to the Kursk offensive were to see Fw 190 serviceability totals in Russia reach their all-time peak – 189 in May and 196 in June 1943. It should be pointed out, moreover, that these figures also include the residual Bf 109s still on the strength of II./JG 54.

If numbers were increasing, so too was Soviet air activity, and with it the opportunity for the *Jagdwaffe* to add to its score. It was in June that Walter Nowotny's star began to ascend, for in that month he achieved 41 kills – his 100th on 15 June, plus 10 in one day on 24 June. Overall, the involvement of JG 54, or *Jagdgeschwader* Trautloft, at this time was pivotal. The latter sobriquet was the name by which the unit had become famous on the Northern Front; the name of the man who had been at their head for nearly three years. The then Major Hannes Trautloft had first taken command of the three previously separate *Gruppen* which made up JG 54 during the Battle of Britain. He had welded them into a single whole, had given them an identity by introducing the famous *Grünherz* badge, in honour of his Thuringian homeland – the Green Heart of Germany – and had been their *Kommodore* ever since.

On 5 July Oberstleutnant Trautloft relinquished command of JG 54 to Major Hubertus von Bonin. Promoted to the position of *Inspizient Ost* (Inspector of Fighters, Eastern Front) on the staff of *General der Jagdflieger* Adolf Galland, Trautloft would continue to keep a paternal eye on the *Jagdgeschwader* with which his name will always be associated.

The the same day Trautloft left JG 54, the long-awaited Operation *Zitadelle*, Hitler's last huge gamble to break the deadlock and turn the tide in the east once and for all, finally commenced. All but one of the five Fw 190 *Jagdgruppen* in the east were directly involved in *Zitadelle*. Leaving just Hauptmann Heinrich Jung's II./JG 54 with its mixed bag of 50 Fw 190s and Bf 109s (38 serviceable) under *Luftflotte* 1 to guard the sectors further to the north, I./JG 54, together with I., III. and IV./JG 51 (140 Fw 190s in all, 88 serviceable) gathered along the northern flank of the salient as the fighter component of *Luftflotte* 6, the Air Fleet tasked with supporting Generaloberst Walter Model's 9th Army.

The first morning of the offensive was occupied in providing bomber and Ju 87 escort, and it was not until the afternoon that the first serious clashes with Soviet fighters took place. Having exchanged their Fw 190A-3s for newer A-4s and -5s just prior to *Zitadelle*, the pilots of JG 51 managed to wrest local air superiority from the Russians for the first few days of the assault. During this period the acknowledged *Experten* all added to their scores. But it was a hitherto unfamiliar name which flared suddenly, and all too briefly, into brilliance over the battlefields of Kursk. 8. *Staffel's* Oberfeldwebel Hubert Strassl, a 24-year-old Austrian, had been with the

Geschwader since late 1941, in which time he had achieved 37 kills. In four separate sorties during the first afternoon and evening of *Zitadelle*, he claimed an amazing 15 more! On the next day he added a further 10. On 7 July it was just two, but on the fourth day the exhausted Strassl's luck finally deserted him. After despatching three more victims, he was himself bounced by four LaGG-3s south of Ponyri. Unable to get out from under his attackers, Strassl found himself being forced ever lower. Then a burst from one of the Russians shredded his wing. Desperately he baled out at less than 1000 ft, but failed to open his parachute in time.

JG 51 were to lose four more pilots during the first five days of *Zitadelle*, but on 10 July events took a more ominous and alarming turn. Aerial opposition was hardening; Russian bomber attacks were on the increase, and their fighters began, for the first time, to mount their own version of the *'Freie Jagd'* sweep over German-held territory. On the ground, the Soviet counter-offensive was launched north of Orel, smashing into 9th Army's rear. The strength of resistance was being reflected in JG 51's losses. By 17 July, when the German assault was broken off, ten more pilots had gone down, including two 30-plus aces: Leutnant Albert Walter and Oberfeldwebel Hans Pfahler of III. and IV. *Gruppe* respectively. On 11 July IV./JG 51 had also lost their *Gruppenkommandeur*, Major Rudolf Resch (94 kills), to fighters south of Ponyri.

Present in only single *Gruppe* strength, JG 54's Kursk casualties were commensurately lighter. But on the second day of the action I./JG 54 also suffered the loss of their *Gruppenkommandeur* when Major Reinhard 'Seppl' Seiler, who had replaced the departed Major Philipp in April, was severely wounded minutes after achieving his 100th victory. At least five more pilots were lost at Kursk, including newcomer, Leutnant Günther Scheel. Having joined 3. *Staffel* in the spring, Scheel had rarely returned from a mission without scoring; amassing 71 kills in about as many sorties. On 17 July Scheel rammed a Yak-9 near Orel and crashed from 700 ft, his Fw 190 exploding on impact. Twenty-four hours later Feldwebel Helmut Missner was able to record the *Geschwader*'s 5000th victory.

But it was in the immediate aftermath of *Zitadelle* that the most grievous losses of all were sustained, among them a quartet of long-serving, highly experienced, formation leaders. Hauptmann Heinrich Jung, who had been promoted from *Staffelkapitän* of 4./JG 54 to take command of II. *Gruppe* after the loss of 'Assi' Hahn, had scored 68 kills before succumbing to Soviet fighters near Mga, southeast of Leningrad, on 30 July. Four days later Major Gerhard Homuth, an ex-Mediterranean Bf 109 ace with 63 victories who had been posted to I./JG 54 on 1 August to fill the vacancy left by 'Seppl' Seiler's recent wounding, failed to return from the Orel area on only his second mission at the head of the *Gruppe*. Stepping into the breach, acting *Gruppenkommandeur* Hans Götz (82 victory *Experte* and *Staffelkapitän* of 2./JG 54) was lost on the very next day – he was last seen going down inverted into woodlands near Karachev after attacking a formation of marauding Il-2s. Finally, Austrian veteran 31-year-old Hauptmann Max Stotz, *Staffelkapitän* of 5./JG 54, also disappeared without trace after baling out over Soviet territory east of Vitebsk on 19 August. With a final total of 189 enemy aircraft destroyed, Stotz is numbered among the top 20 highest scoring Luftwaffe aces of the war.

Still concentrated along the northern flank of the dwindling salient, JG

Despite leading a seemingly endless succession of sorties over the huge battle front at Kursk Hauptmann Erich Rudorffer, *Gruppenkommandeur* of II./JG 54, still manages to raise a smile as he enjoys a quick cigarette between ops at Orel on 28 August 1943. Rudorffer ended the war with a staggering total of 222 kills, 136 of which were claimed on the Russian Front. His final dozen kills were achieved with the Me 262 whilst serving as *Gruppenkommandeur* of II./JG 7

51's three *Gruppen* also continued to suffer attrition in the days and weeks which followed the abandonment of the Kursk offensive. Lying in the very path of the Soviet counter-attack, their losses were not just restricted to pilots; an increasing number of groundcrew were being killed by Russian bomber and *Stormovik* raids on the airfields at and around Orel. Austrian skier Leutnant Josef 'Pepi' Jennewein, to whom real success had only come after I. *Gruppe*'s conversion to the Fw 190, and whose tally now stood at 86, was lost at this time. He finally met his match east of Orel on 26 July. Twelve days later Hauptmann Heinrich Höfemeier of 3./JG 51, who was just four kills short of his 100, was lost to flak near Krachev.

But for the *Jagdwaffe* the real repercussions of the failure at Kursk were far wider reaching than individual unit losses, as swingeing as these had been. Although the initial Soviet counter-thrust had been halted at great cost just short of Orel, the respite was short-lived. Sixty-one Soviet armies lay coiled behind their frontline, and in August Stalin unleashed them in a series of smashing blows. To the north of Kursk the offensive was renewed not just against Orel, but now also against Yelnya, Smolensk and Velizh as well. To the south Kharkov and Poltava were threatened; further south still, Stalino and the entire Ukraine. Only the 12 armies opposite the Northern Sector still remained relatively dormant. And this time the Soviet offensives would not be halted; not by the Germans, not by the weather. Maintaining their pressure throughout the winter, they would continue until the spring of 1944.

This entire eight-month period was one of unparalleled movement for the Fw 190 *Gruppen* of JG 51 and JG 54 as an increasingly hard pressed General Staff shuffled them around on their headquarters operations maps like so many chessmen from one new breach along the endangered 700 mile front to the next. For not only were the Russians growing stronger by the day, the *Jagdwaffe*'s Eastern Front strength was continually being eroded.

The seven *Jagdgeschwader* which had accompanied the launching of *Barbarossa* two summers ago had since been reduced to four by the demands of the Mediterranean fronts. Now it was the defence of the *Reich* which needed shoring up. And the result? The departure of another *Jagdgeschwader*, leaving just three – in theory, one neatly allocated to each of the sectors, North, Central and South – to stand in the way of the greatest advance in military history.

Nor was it simply in numbers that home-defence took precedence. The reality of US heavy bombers actually parading their might deeper into *Reich* airspace had focussed the collective Berlin mind wonderfully. And the supply of new Fw 190s to the far flung, low priority, reaches of Russia – never good at the best of times – became positively precarious. The first *Jagdgruppe* to suffer, Major Hans-Ekkehard Bob's IV./JG 51, had already perforce reverted to the Bf 109G-6. Others would follow. But before tracing the fortunes of the remaining Fw 190-equipped *Gruppen* as they embarked upon their long retreat, it is necessary to go back to the start of *Zitadelle* . . . this time to the southern flank.

SCHLACHTFLIEGER

While JGs 51 and 54 had been engaged along the northern flank of the Kursk salient, the southern extremities had been similarly covered by their Bf 109-equipped counterparts, JGs 3 and 52 (the former being the unit soon to be recalled to Defence of the Reich duties). There *was* an Fw 190 presence in the south as well, however, in the form of two *Gruppen* – some 40 plus aircraft in all – currently being employed as bombers!

The evolution of the Luftwaffe's ground-attack arm was a protracted and complicated process. It began simply enough on the outbreak of war with a single *Gruppe* of ageing Hs 123 biplanes operating under the not-so-simple designation of II.(*Schl.*)/LG 2 [2nd (Ground-attack) Wing of the 2nd Instructional and Development Group]. Having wrought surprising havoc in the close-support rôle across Poland and through France, this *Gruppe* then came to an abrupt halt. Its biplanes too vulnerable to be exposed to direct cross-Channel confrontation with the Hurricanes and Spitfires of RAF Fighter Command, it retired instead to the homeland for re-equipment with the Bf 109. The onus of carrying the *Blitzkrieg* into England would be shouldered by the hitherto invincible Ju 87 alone. But the latter was soon found sadly wanting in the historic air battle that followed; a truth tacitly admitted by Reichsmarschall Hermann Göring when he ordered that a third of all his single-engined fighter strength in the Pas de Calais be converted to carry bombs in place of the Stukas.

Having set a precedent, these early bomb-carrying Bf 109s were subsequently formed into specialised *Jabostaffeln* (fighter-bomber squadrons); in turn to be reorganised, togther with Bf 110s, into *Schnellkampfgeschwader* (fast bomber groups). And the successful conclusion of yet another land *Blitzkrieg*, this time against Yugoslavia, had also restored confidence in both the Stuka and in the ground-attack, or *Schlacht*, Hs 123, with which II.(*Schl.*)/LG 2 was again partially equipped.

This then was the somewhat confusing triumvirate of *Luftwaffe* tactical air support – *Schnellkampf, Stuka* and *Schlacht* – which accompanied the initial ground advances into Russia. By 1942 the single *Schlachtgruppe* of 1939 had expanded into two full *Schlachtgeschwader*, operating a mix of predominantly Bf 109Es with a leavening of Hs 123s and twin-engined Hs 129s. Towards the end of that year, however, the increasing rigours of the Eastern Front were proving that the Bf 109's weaknesses made it even less suitable as a *Schlacht* aircraft than it was as a fighter in the often primitive conditions encountered in the Soviet Union. And when a replacement was sought – a machine that was

II./Schl.G 1 converted to Fw 190F-2s at Deblin-Irena, Poland, in March 1943. This aircraft carries the unit's famous Mickey Mouse badge on its cowling, with its backgound colour in red to denote its assignment to 5.*Staffel* – the prop boss and fuselage code letter were also sprayed red. All of these would be leeched of their colour and left in black prior to the *Staffel*'s return to the front

An impressive line up of pristine II./Schl.G 1 Fw 190Fs

Hauptmann Hans Stollnberger, *Staffelkapitän* of 6./Schl.G 1 at Kursk. He spent four days in Russia behind enemy lines during the battle following a forced landing, and only escaped by swimming the River Don under the cover of darkness. Stollnberger ended the war as *Kapitän* of 8./SG 10 with 45 victories

robust, reliable, handled well at low altitudes and could absorb punishment – the choice was obvious. The first ground-attack unit in the East to be re-equipped with the Fw 190 was Major Hubertus Hitschhold's *Schlachtgeschwader* 1 (Schl.G.1), whose two component *Gruppen* of Bf 109Es began withdrawing one *Staffel* at a time from the River Chir sector of the Stalingrad front in the late autumn of 1942.

The comments of the pilots upon their introduction to the Focke-Wulf were remarkably similar to those of their fighter brethren. Leutnant Fritz Seyffardt of II./Schl.G.1, one of the first to fly the Fw 190 operationally on the Eastern Front and who would end the war with 30 aerial victories:

'In 1942, I saw and flew my first Fw 190; I was thrilled with this machine. During the war I flew the Fw 190A, F and G models, and also the Messerschmitt Bf 109. The difference between the Fw 190 and the Bf 109 was that there was more room in the Focke-Wulf's cockpit and the controls were simpler – for example, landing flaps and trim were electric. Another pronounced difference was the stability of the Fw 190. Thanks to its through-wing spars and wide landing gear the machine was substantially more stable in flight, and especially in landing on rough fields. At great height, engine performance was inadequate. Normal range of the later F models was approximately 375 - 425 miles. The average mission on the Russian Front lasted 45 - 60 minutes. Firepower was very good. As a rule we had two 20 mm cannon and two machine guns. There was also provision for two additional 20 mm cannon in the outer wing panels. As a flying tactic, we had the greatest success when we flew in open formation, in other words with approximately 80 to 100 metres separation between aircraft. In the target area we split into two-plane *Rotte* elements for the attack, only re-assembling into larger formations on the return flight. In altogether about 500 frontline missions, I had to make several belly landings on differing terrains, something that could be done without undue difficulty.'

A similar view, albeit with some reservations, was expressed by Feldwebel Peter Taubel, who first flew the Fw 190 with II./Schl.G.2 in the Mediterranean, before transferring to the Eastern Front:

'The Fw 190 as an aircraft was very advanced. The wide landing gear gave better tracking stability than with the Bf 109. The pilot's seat was comfortable, and armour protection was adequate. Instruments were easily scanned, a fact which pleased me on my first flight in the 190. I found myself very quickly at home. During combat we feared the great risk of fire from being hit. I remember that a fellow pilot burned in his cockpit when he was hit in the fuel system. The inside of his plane instantly burst into flames. Our heavy loading was also a problem. The Fw 190 was very cumbersome at full gross weight.'

Unteroffizier Fritz Kreitl, another later transferee from the Mediterranean theatre, was even less enthusiastic:

'Although the Fw 190 was a fine aircraft, it was not built for fighter-bombing. With 1000 lb of bombs or wing rockets, it performed sluggishly. Thus, take-off and landing with heavy loads forced us to re-write the manual. Landing speeds were increased by nearly 15 mph and when we were posted to the north Russian Front we were confronted with other hazards. The howling albino hell of the Russian winter made flying and maintenance a nightmare. In order to keep our engines from freezing up, fires were often built beneath them. Starts were accomplished in 20 degrees below zero weather by filling the sump with ¾ gasoline and ¼ oil. When you ignited this mixture, the gasoline would burn off immediately, heating the oil; one check of the mags, and a quick rev of the engine and you were up and flying. The cockpit of the Fw 190 was roomy, but forward vision on landing and take-off was nil, and the pilot could not see the ground either when lifting off or prior to touchdown. The aircraft's climb was outstanding and one of the best ways to leave an attacker was to haul back on the stick and point straight up. Although it turned well, the Focke-Wulf had the same tendency to skid in a turn as did the Bf 109. In a turn, the Fw 190 had an alarming, almost frightening penchant when the stick was sucked all the way back. In a tight right-hand turn, the aircraft would flip on its back and go down. Right rudder would escalate this and if you were being pursued, this disengaging manoeuvre was certain to

One of the Luftwaffe's most experienced *Schlachtflieger* was Major Alfred Druschel, *Geschwaderkommodore* of Schl.G 1. Note his Oak Leaves and Swords, awarded on 19 February 1943 for completing 700 mission. He was killed over the Ardennes during Operation *Bodenplatte* on New Year's Day 1945

A 'black man' catches 40 winks alongside a *Stab* machine of the *Gefechtsverband* Druschel (Schl.G 1) during the hot summer of 1943. Note the mechanic's standard issue toolbox to his left

The *Schlachtfliegers'* principal targets at Kursk were tanks, and the Russians certainly provided them with plenty of targets. Near Rzhev no less than 45 T-34s were destroyed from the air by II./Schl.G 1, their charred remains serving as testament to the firepower of the ground-attack configured Fw 190

If T-34s proved vulnerable to the prowling Fw 190s, then soft-skinned vehicles stood no chance at all. This is all that remains of just one of 46 trucks blown apart by II./Schl.G 1 again at Rzhev

throw your enemy off. However, it was not recommended under 3000 ft. You needed that much altitude to recover, and at high speeds the G-forces were immense, often causing the blood vessels in the eye to burst.'

Although the first *Staffeln* of Schl.G.1 had returned to the Southern Sector of the front early in 1943, where they helped to cover the first stages of the withdrawal from the Caucasus, the *Geschwader* did not complete re-equipment with the Fw 190 until May; just in time for the build-up to *Zitadelle*. The part played by Schl.G.1's two *Gruppen* of Fw 190s in the Battle of Kursk has always been overshadowed by the specialised tank-buster units equipped with cannon-armed versions of the Ju 87 and Hs 129. For while the latter targeted the Soviet armour, the Fw 190s' primary job was to attack its supporting infantry and the Russian artillery positions with SD-1 and -2 anti-personnel cluster bombs. These were containers which scattered either 180 or 360 small fragmentation bombs over a wide area with devastating effect. But for the pilots of Schl.G.1, commanded now by Major Alfred Druschel and based for the Kursk assault at Varvarovka, the Red Army's response to their attacks was an eye-opener. In contrast to the German habit of promptly hitting the dirt and relying upon their accompanying flak to deal with low-flying aircraft, it was observed that, 'with the Russians, everyone and everything shoots back!' One famous contemporary comment describes the hail of fire encountered over Kursk even more graphically: 'They just blazed away with everything they'd got; machine guns, rifles, even pistols. The amount of iron in the air was indescribable. I swear, they would have thrown horseshoes at us, if they could have got them off the horses in time.' It did not augur well for future *Schlacht* operations.

After the German attack was called off in mid-July, the Fw 190s of I. and II./Schl.G 1 began to concentrate more and more on the Russian lines of supply which were bringing up the men and equipment needed to sustain the massive Soviet counter offensive. They enjoyed considerable success against these soft-skinned targets, as typified by the following report:

'On 11 July I was leading my *Schwarm* towards Kursk. We were

flying at about 1500 metres, well spread out in battle formation. A beautiful summer's day, not an enemy fighter in the sky, and below us a supply road - at first without any traffic on it. But look there, a column of trucks heading south, huge clouds of tell-tale dust, they were certainly in a hurry. About a dozen trucks in all, each heavily laden with fuel drums. I split my *Schwarm* into two *Rotten* and gave the order for a low-level attack. My *Rotte* took the head of the convoy, attacking from the flank; the other began from the tail end. After the first pass one or two trucks were already well alight. We were in luck. We'd caught a fuel convoy and could destroy it at our leisure – no fighters around and the ground defences were minimal. After 15 minutes nothing remained but a dozen blazing wrecks, and smoke climbed some 500-700 metres into the air. There were targets galore for us ground-attack units. We certainly couldn't complain.'

However, such individual attacks were pin-pricks against the flood-tide of advancing Soviets. A month after Kursk II./Schl.G 1 had retired to the area of Kharkov. The above report continues:

'Despite every effort, our ground forces were unable to stop the Red Army's onslaught. The road to Kharkov ran alongside our new base at Kharkov-Rogan. It was full of our infantry heading westwards. Our groundcrews asked the soldiers what their orders were, where they were heading for, only to be told that they were the division's rearguard and that the next lot of troops coming down the road would be Russian! We pilots were none too pleased at this news. We told our chief, who in turn informed the *Gruppenkommandeur* of the situation. All hell broke loose. Within the hour we had transferred lock, stock and barrel to Bol-Rudka, a field north of Poltava. Nobody had thought to let our *Gruppe* know what was happening. That same day Rogan was overrun by the Russians. But we had managed to save our machines, equipment and ground staff without loss. The Ju 52 crews, as so often during this period, were right on the spot. Without the help of the transport *Staffeln* we Eastern Front flyers could have simply disappeared without trace on many an occasion.

'Bol-Rudka was just a field which had been turned into a landing strip. We arrived like a travelling circus and set up shop. Everybody knew what he had to do, and soon we were flying missions to the north and northeast. The exact location of our front lines was unknown. Our first job was to pin-point the positions of our forward troops. Many had been cut off behind the advancing Russians. Enemy spearheads were pushing deep to the south and south-west. One thing was certain, they had broken through our front in many places and were pouring into our rear.

'Our groundcrews were magnificent. We were flying from first light until late evening. Our main task was to attack Ivan's armour and his supply lines. Our local successes were colossal, but we couldn't stop the overall momentum of the advance. It was also becoming obvious that the *Stukageschwader* with their Ju 87s were no longer up to the conditions we were having to face by the autumn of 1943.'

Locomotives also proved highlt desirable targets for marauding *Schlachtflieger*, as this engine found out to its cost. An impressive tally of 47 locos was claimed destroyed by II./Schl.G 1 at the time of the Kursk offensive

A suitably chuffed Oberfeldwebel Hermann Buchner receives the accolades of his groundcrew following the successful completion of his 300th operational sortie at Bol-Rudka on 27 August 1943

Living quarters in the south didn't run to Czars' palaces, as enjoyed by the *Jagdflieger* on the Leningrad Front. II./Schl.G 1 had to make do with tents, or even holes in the ground. Steel helmet perched on the lip of his fox hole, a young *Schlachtflieger* practices his accordian in between sorties. The exposed nature of this accommodation on the Crimean plain can be easily seen from this snapshot

When II./Schl.G 1's 'lavish' complex of holes in the ground at Tusow was overrun by sand vipers in late summer 1943, only Unteroffizier Lebsanft, seen here, saved the day as he proved to be extremely adept at catching these poisonous reptiles. He was duly crowned the *Gruppe's* champion viper catcher!

In fact, one result of the failure at Kursk was the long-overdue restructuring of the Luftwaffe's ground-attack and close-support formations. Until this time all *Stukagruppen* had been part of the bomber arm and were controlled by the *General der Kampfflieger*, whereas the *Schlacht-* and *Schnellkampfgruppen*, although not 'fighters' in the strict sense of the meaning, had nonetheless found themselves operating under the aegis of the *General der Jagdflieger*. With effect from 18 October 1943, all three branches were combined into a new and separate ground-attack arm of the Luftwaffe under the command of a *General der Schlachtflieger*. As of this date all existing *Stukageschwader* (St.Gs 1, 2, 3, 5 and 77), with the exception of two *Gruppen*, were officially redesignated *Schlachtgeschwader* (henceforth to be abbreviated to the simpler SG).

Of the original pair of *Schlachtgeschwader*, Schl.G.1's two component *Gruppen* were used to fill the gaps in the newly created SGs left by the two *Gruppen* referred to above (II./St.G 2 and I./St.G 77) which initially retained their *Stuka* designations and continued to operate semi-autonomously as dive-bomber units. Thus I. and II./Schl.G.1 joined the ranks of the SGs as I./SG 77 and II./SG 2 respectively. Meanwhile the *Gruppen* of Schl.G.2, together with those of SKG 10, were amalgamated, via a convoluted series of redesignations, into two new *Schlachtgeschwader*, emerging as SGs 4 and 10.

Despite the new nomenclature, the bulk of the ex-*Stuka*, now *Schlacht, Geschwader* continued to fly their Ju 87s. The pressing and ever-growing need for Fw 190s in the Homeland and the West meant that the SGs on the Russian Front – still very much the poor relation in terms of aircraft allocation – would not begin converting on to the Focke-Wulf until the spring of 1944. It also meant that the conversion programme itself would be a long drawn out affair. Conducted on a *Gruppe* by *Gruppe* basis, it would eventually degenerate from a 6-8 week course somewhere in a rear area for those fortunate enough to undergo 'early' transition and re-equipment, into a few circuits and bumps, plus some 15-20 sorties flying as wingman to a more experienced pilot while remaining on operations , which is all that the final few to forsake the Ju 87 for the Fw 190 would enjoy, before the whole programme ground to a halt in January 1945.

And so, with the Fw 190-equipped SGs 10 and 4 not transferring in from the Mediterranean to Russia until the end of 1943 and mid-1944 respectively, it fell to the two original *Schlachtgruppen* from the Battle of Kursk – now operating as I./SG 77 and II./SG 2 – to remain as the Eastern Front's only Fw 190 ground-attack presence for the rest of the year. Fielding a combined total of something less than 40 serviceable machines between them for most of that time, there was little they could do to halt the advance of 13 Soviet armies south-westwards towards the Black Sea.

Here's one for the experts. According to the original Russian caption, this somewhat battered Fw 190 conveniently providing a perch for a couple of young goatherds came down near Glukhov, in the Ukraine, in September 1943. The vertical bar aft of the cross denotes a III.*Gruppe* machine, but the 'White O' in old-fashioned German script is not exactly regulation! Did III./JG 51 perhaps have an individualist among its numbers?

By the beginning of January 1944 the *Gruppe* which had had to vacate Kharkov-Rogan for Bol-Rudka in such a hurry the previous August had been pushed back even further. They now found themselves on Malaya-Whisky, the oddly named forward landing strip located to the west of Kirovograd, which they shared with the Bf 109Gs of II./JG 52. Here, in their new guise as II./SG 2, they had an even closer shave. *Oberfeldwebel* Hermann Buchner takes up the story from where he left off in the autumn:

'By now it was deep winter and weather conditions were not exactly good. Visibility was a few kilometres at best, overcast with light snow showers. Our position wasn't exactly rosy either. Ivan's tanks had broken through at Kirovograd. The road leading south-westwards was packed with his armour and supply columns in division strength. We had our hands full. Continual low-level attacks, supported by a *Stukagruppe* and covered by the Bf 109s of II./JG 52. We were flying from morning till night and were very unpopular with Ivan. The consequences weren't long in coming. On the night of 13 January a force of enemy tanks managed to break through to our field.

'About midnight the alarm sounded and the adjutant woke the pilots. We were housed in the village school and were ordered to

Below and bottom The first snowfall of the impending winter catches two II./SG 2 machines (below) bombed up and ready for their next sortie from the flat expanse of the steppes. Note the tropical filter on the *Gruppen-Adjutant's* machine in the left foreground – this won't be needed for much longer as the summer's dust gives way to snow. The temporary nature of facilities in this region is graphically brought home bya close examination of the bottom photograph

Yet to receive their winter coats, a scattered group of *Schlact* Fw 190Fs sit quietly nestling their bombs, awaiting the appearance of pilots from tents or foxholes in late 1943

make our own way to the field and assemble at the *Staffel* dispersals. Russian T-34s with infantry aboard were in the village and had overrun the eastern edge of the field where II./JG 52 were dispersed. Eight 109s had had their tails crushed by enemy tanks rolling over them. Another T-34 had driven over the roof of their ops room bunker and fallen through into the trench below. The field's mobile quadruple 20 mm flak guns were engaging the Russian infantry. We pilots and groundcrew alike found ourselves on the western perimeter of the field. We were ordered to prepare our 190s and technical equipment for demolition should Ivan manage to overrun our area too. The signal would be a green flare from the *Gruppe* main ops room. After that we were to make our way westwards on foot. It was a pitch-black night and freezing cold. At about 3 in the morning a dim figure approached. It was the acting *Kommandeur* of the 109 *Gruppe,* Hauptmann Sepp Haiböck, who informed us that most of his aircraft had been flattened by the enemy's tanks.

'Our own 20 mm flak vehicles drove off into the darkness to join the

Above and right What the well-dressed Fw 190F wore in the depths of winter. Heating trollies and tents were available only for the lucky few! The latter were often reserved for aircraft undergoing in-the-field maintenance, as conditions often proved too bitter in the depths of winter for 'black men' to work outdoors for any period of time. Note that 'White N' has had a toned down cross applied to its fuselage, although its overall effect is spoiled somewhat by the full-colour *Staffel* markings

fight on the eastern edge of the field. The base's heavier 88 mm flak guns began to engage the T-34s with some success. We just stood around, frozen stiff and waiting for orders. Towards dawn the sounds of battle from across the field began to diminish. At first light a trio of He 111s roared in at low-level with the obvious intention of bombing us - they must have thought the field had been captured. We were able to stop them at the last minute by shooting off recognition flares. Then came the Stukas, looking for

targets around the eastern perimeter. We had a ringside view as one of them was shot down by a Russian anti-aircraft tank. But fortunately the crew managed to parachute to safety.

'It had been a hectic night. And it wasn't over yet. At about 10.00 hours our flak, supported by some mounted infantry from the village, managed to seal the breach. All the enemy tanks were destroyed, and his infantry either killed or taken prisoner. We could breathe again. Our 190s were undamaged. But JG 52's 109s had all been lost, and one unfortunate HQ clerk had been crushed by the T-34 falling into the ops dugout.

'By mid-day it was business as usual. The *Kommandeur* issued new orders. For me this meant taking a group of pilots to collect four new 190s from the depot at Uman.'

Shortly after this II./SG 2 retired to the Crimea, based first at Karankut and then sharing Cherson-South with the Bf 109s of II./JG 52 again. The severity of the recent fighting had reduced the *Jagdgruppe*'s serviceable strength to single figures. And so, in addition to their continuing ground-attack missions, the Fw 190A-5/U1s of II./SG 2 found themselves becoming embroiled in the battle for air supremacy over the beleaguered Crimean bridgehead. 6. *Staffel*'s Oberfeldwebel Hermann Buchner here recalls a typical operation of this period, ordered to be flown by a mixed *Schwarm* of two Fw 190s and two Bf 109s:

'Shortly before 11.00 hours we taxied out for take-off. Unfortunately, my wingman did not spot a fresh bomb crater and completed his mission there and then standing on his nose. I reached the take-off point somewhat late myself, to find only a single Bf 109 waiting for me. Obviously his wingman had had some difficulties too!

'The Bf 109 had two black chevrons on his fuselage (presumably indicating the aircraft, if not the actual presence, of II./JG 52's *Gruppenkommandeur*, Hauptmann Gerhard Barkhorn, who, with a final total of 301 victories, was to become the world's number two ranking ace of all time, second only to the legendary Erich Hartmann). The pilot signalled that he would fly as leader. We took off westwards, and I soon discovered that my Fw 190 could more than hold its own against the Bf 109.

'We were some 1000 metres above the Black Sea when the first message came through from ground control: "*Indianer* in harbour area *SEWA; Hanni* 3-4." ("Bandits over Sevastopol harbour, height 3000 - 4000 metres").

'My *Schwarmführer* continued to climb while I covered his tail and kept a careful watch for bandits. We were soon flying at 4000 metres approaching Sevastopol from the west. Then we spotted them, somewhat lower: enemy fighters. The *Schwarmführer*'s voice crackled over my headphones: "*Pauke, Pauke!*" ("Tally-Ho!").

'He dived into the attack, scattering the enemy fighters. They were Yaks and we twisted and turned among them for about ten minutes without scoring a single kill. Then they broke away. Ground control quickly came back on air: "Fly to Balaclava area, large formation of Il-2s and *Indianer*."

'The Bf 109 reduced speed and its pilot indicated that I should take over the lead. Now I was in front with the Messerschmitt protecting my tail. We were soon approaching Balaclava and could see the smoke-bursts of our own flak. Another wild dogfight with Yak-9s began, and this time

Karankut, in the Crimea. A combat-weary Hermann Buchner celebrates his 500th mission in March 1944

II./SG 2's *Gruppe* ops bunker at Cherson in April 1944 is the meeting place for Oberleutnant Ernst Beutelspacher (right), *Staffelkapitän* of 6./SG 2, and an anonymous pliot from his *Staffel*. The former would be awarded the Knight's Cross the following month, only to be killed in action against US fighters over Rumania in July

The most successful *Schlachtflieger* in terms of aerial kills was 5./SG 2's Leutnant August Lambert, pictured here in the Crimea in May 1944. By the time he was killed in April 1945, Lambert had downed 116 aircraft

Hermann Buchner's 600th op is celebrated barely two months after his 500th at Bacau, in Rumania, in early June 1944. He is flanked in front of his Fw 190F-8 'Green Y' by his chief mechanic (at the back on the right) and his *'Katschmarek'* (left), a fresh-faced youngster named Wolfgang von Richthofen, son of the famous General Wolfram von Richthofen of the early Stuka days. Gefreiter von Richthofen was reported missing in action in Fw 190 'Green G' over Jasy, Rumania, on 5 June 1944

Oberfeldwebel Buchner pictured after the award of the Knight's Cross on 20 July 1944. Although not visible in this view, Buchner also wore the *Deutsches Kreuz* (German Cross) on the right breast pocket, and a ground-attack clasp and pennant, pilot's badge, wound badge and the Crimea shield on his left sleeve

I was able to bring one down. It crashed to the ground in flames. The rest of the *Indianer* broke for the east. Far below us the Il-2s were attacking our ground positions north of Balaclava. Quickly losing height, we dived on the enemy *Stormoviks* from astern. After a few bursts I managed to get an Il-2. His port wing erupted in flames. He tipped over and smashed into the ground.'

The above victories were but two of Hermann Buchner's final tally of 58 enemy aircraft destroyed. Having first joined II./Schl.G.1 in February 1942, his subsequent career was nothing if not spectacular. Shot down five times, he twice baled out and was twice wounded. On the Eastern Front he claimed 46 kills, plus the same number of tanks and one armoured train destroyed. Awarded the Knight's Cross and commissioned, Leutnant Buchner ended the war flying the Me 262 in Defence of the Reich duties, shooting down 12 four-engined bombers, and being nominated for the Oak Leaves in the process.

But during the closing stages of the Crimean campaign there was one member of II./SG 2 whose exploits eclipsed all others. It is claimed that some 604 Soviet aircraft were brought down during the six months' fighting leading up to the final German evacuation of the Crimea. Of that total an astounding 247 had fallen to the Fw 190s of II./SG 2. More amazing still, one man alone accounted for over a third of the *Schlacht-gruppe's* victories. 5.*Staffel's* Leutnant August Lambert amassed over 70 kills in just three weeks, scoring as many as 12, 14 and 17 in a single day! He was awarded the Knight's Cross in May 1944 when he had 90 victories to his credit. After the fall of the Crimea Lambert went back to instructing, a job he had been doing prior to his posting to II./Schl.G 1 in April 1943. He was to return to the front in the final weeks of the war, only to fall victim to American Mustangs. His final total stood at 116 enemy aircraft destroyed – all gained on the Eastern Front – making him the highest scoring *Schlachtflieger* of them all.

Having been bottled up on the Crimea for over four months, II./SG 2 retired westwards across the Black Sea to Rumania early in May 1944. They were initially based at Bacau, a field they shared with I./SG 10. For, at long last, the ex-Stuka re-equipment programme was finally beginning

Buchner shares a joke with two members of his *Schwarm* after surviving yet another sortie over Rumania in mid-1944. Note the extreme variation in clothing

Buchner's chief mechanic Unteroffizier Wiezorek, poses in the spring slush in front of 'his' Fw 190F-8

to make itself felt. There were seven Fw 190-equipped *Schlachtgruppen* deployed on the Southern and Central Sectors of the Eastern Front. The ex-Mediterranean SG 10 was present in no less than full three *Gruppe* strength. I. and II./SG 10 were both in Rumania with II./SG 2. In southern Poland III./SG 10 was grouped alongside I./SG 77 (the original I./Schl.G 1) and the newly converted II./SG 77. On the Central Sector there was as yet just the one *Gruppe* fully re-equipped with the Fw 190 – III./SG 1.

This 'build-up' (between them the seven *Gruppen* fielded 197 serviceable Fw 190s in May; a more than three-fold increase on the previous month's figure) was timely. The series of Soviet counter-offensives which had followed on from the German retreat at Kursk had finally halted. But the respite was to be only temporary. In June Stalin would launch his massive Belorussian offensive which would take the Red Army to the eastern borders of Germany itself.

The burgeoning strength of the *Schlacht* arm may have been cause for cautious optimism, even at this late stage of the war in the east. But what of the Fw 190 fighter presence on the main Soviet fronts post-Kursk? By that same June 1944, when it was estimated that Soviet air power stood at nearly 13,500 aircraft, the number of serviceable Focke-Wulfs would have sunk to an incredible all-time low of just 31!

The losses – Oberleutnant Beutelspacher (left) and Leutnant Lambert (right), were both *Schlachtflieger* Knight's Cross holders and were both killed by US fighters. They are seen here in their respective finery in Rumania in 1944

Pilots of II./SG 2 shot down by marauding USAAF P-38 Lightnings over Czechoslovakia are buried at Prossnitz in 1944. By this stage in the war the military cemeteries were rapidly filling up with downed *Schlachtflieger*

COLOUR PLATES

This 18-page section profiles many of the aircraft flown by Lufwaffe Fw 190 aces of the Russian Front. The majority of these aircraft have never been seen in colour before, and the shear breadth of variation in camouflage schemes is quite fascinating, as is the general lack of unit markings or rudder scoreboards.

As is always the case in this ever-growing series, the artworks have all been specially commissioned for this volume, and author/artist John Weal, plus figure artist Mike Chappell, has gone to great pains to illustrate the aircraft, and their pilots, as accurately as possible following much original in-depth research.

1
Fw 190A-8 'Black Double Chevron', flown by Hauptmann Paul-Heinrich Dähne, Gruppenkommandeur II./JG 1, Mecklenburg, circa February 1945

2
Fw 190A-8 'Yellow 1', flown by Major Bernd Gallowitsch, Staffelkapitän 7./JG 1, Garz/Usedom, March 1945

3
Fw 190D-9 'Black Double Chevron', flown by Oberleutnant Oskar Romm, Gruppenkommandeur IV./JG 3, Prenzlau, March 1945

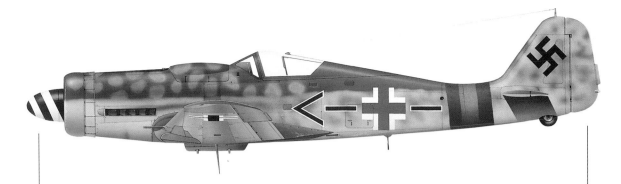

4
Fw 190D-9 'Black Chevron and Bars', flown by Oberstleutnant Gerhard Michalski, Geschwaderkommodore JG 4, Oder Front, circa January 1945

5
Fw 190A-3 'Black 1', flown by Hauptmann Friedrich-Wilhelm Strakeljahn, Staffelkapitän 14. (Jabo)/JG 5, Petsamo/northern Finland, circa June 1943

6
Fw 190D-9 'Black Chevron and Bars, flown by Major Gerhard Barkhorn, Geschwaderkommodore JG 6, Lower Silesia, circa January 1945

7
Fw 190A-8 'Black Double Chevron', flown by Hauptmann Herbert Kutscha, Gruppenkommandeur III./JG 11, Brandenburg, circa February 1945

8
Fw 190A-3 'Black Double Chevron', flown by Hauptmann Heinrich Krafft Gruppenkommandeur I./JG 51, Jesau/East Prussia, August 1942

9
Fw 190-A-5 'Black Double Chevron', flown by Major Erich Leie, Gruppenkommandeur I./JG 51, Orel, Circa May 1943

10
Fw 190A-3 'Black Double Chevron', flown by Hauptmann Rudolf Busch, Gruppenkommandeur I./JG 51, Lake Ivan/Russia, January 1943

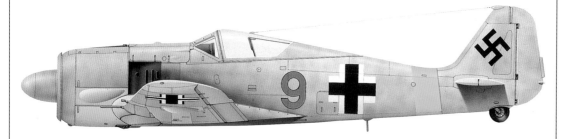

11
Fw 190A-3 'Yellow 9', flown by Hauptmann Heinz Lange, Staffelkapitän 3./JG 51, Vyazma, December 1942

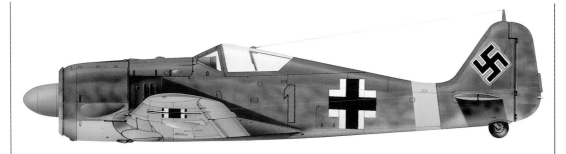

12
Fw 190A-4 'Yellow 1, flown by Oberfeldwebel Herbert Bareuther, 3./JG 51,
Orel, June 1943

13
Fw 190A-4 'Yellow 5', flown by Leutnant Josef Jennewein, 3./JG 51,
Orel, June 1943

14
Fw 190A-5 'Black Double Chevron', flown by Hauptmann Fritz Losigkeit, Gruppenkommandeur III./JG 51,
Kursk, July 1943

15
Fw 190A-3 'White 11', flown by Hauptmann Herbert Wehnelt, Staffelkapitän 7./JG 51,
Orel, circa January 1943

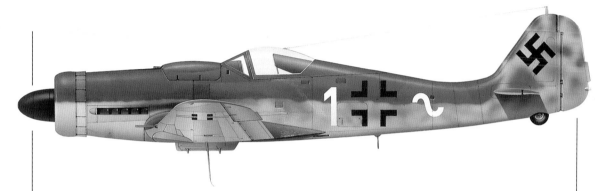

16
Fw 190D-9 'White 1', flown by Leutnant Kurt Tanzer, Staffelkapitän 13./JG 51,
Schmoldow/Pomerania, April 1945

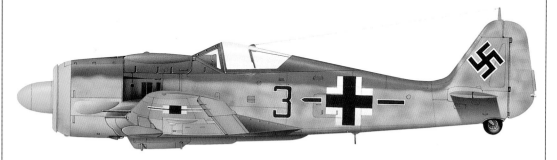

17
Fw 190A-8 'Black 3 and Bars', flown by Unteroffizier Helmut Johne, Stabsstaffel JG 51,
Memel, November 1944

18
Fw 190A-8 'Black 6 and Bars', flown by Oberfeldwebel Fritz Lüddecke, Stabsstaffel JG 51,
Orscha, circa July 1944

19
Fw 190A-8 'Black 11 and Bars', flown by Leutnant Günther Heym, Stabsstaffel JG 51,
Zichenau, circa September 1944

20
Fw 190A-8 'Black 12 and Bars', flown by Feldwebel Johann Merbeler, Stabsstaffel JG 51,
Neukuhren/East Prussia, November 1944

21
Fw 190A-4 'Black Double Chevron and Bars', flown by Oberstleutnant Hannes Trautloft, Geschwaderkommodore JG 54,
Krasnogvardeisk, circa December 1942

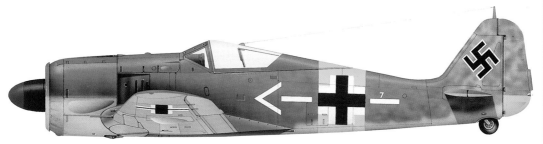

22
Fw 190A-4 'White Chevron and Bars', flown by Major Hubertus von Bonin, Geschwaderkommodore JG 54,
Krasnogvardeisk, circa August 1943

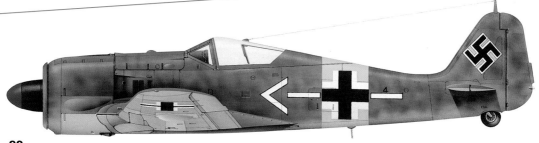

23
Fw 190A-5 'White Chevron and Bars', flown by Major Hubertus von Bonin, Geschwaderkommodore JG 54,
Central Sector, circa November 1943

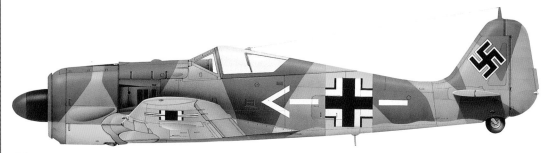

24
Fw 190A-6 'White Chevron and Bars, flown by Oberstleutnant Anton Mader, Geschwaderkommodore JG 54, Dorpat/Estonia, July 1944

25
Fw 190A-4 'Black Double Chevron', flown by Hauptmann Hans Philipp, Gruppenkommandeur I./JG 54, Krasnogvardeisk, circa January 1943

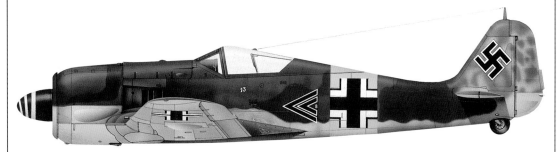

26
Fw 190A-6 'Black Double Chevron', flown by Hauptmann Walter Nowotny, Gruppenkommandeur I./JG 54, Vitebsk, November 1943

27
Fw 190A-8 'Black Double Chevron', flown by Hauptmann Franz Eisenach, Gruppenkommandeur I./JG 54, Schrunden/Courland, circa November 1944

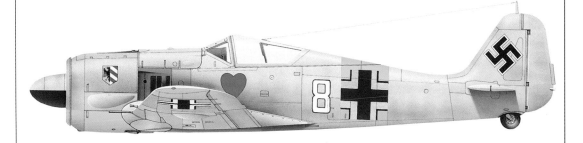

28
Fw 190A-4 'White 8', flown by Leutnant Walter Nowotny, Staffelkapitän 1./JG 54,
Krasnogvardeisk, November 1942

29
Fw 190A-4 'White 10', flown by Leutnant Walter Nowotny, Staffelkapitän 1./JG 54,
Krasnogvardeisk, Spring 1943

30
Fw 190A-5 'White 5', flown by Oberleutnant Walter Nowotny, Staffelkapitän 1./JG 54,
Krasnogvardeisk, circa June 1943

31
Fw 190A-6 'White 12', flown by Leutnant Helmut Wettstein, Staffelkapitän 1./JG 54,
Central Sector, circa 1943

32
Fw 190A-8 'White 1', flown by Leutnant Heinz Wernicke, Staffelkapitän 1./JG 54,
Riga-Skulte/Latvia, circa September 1944

33
Fw 190A-8 'White 12', flown by Oberleutnant Josef Heinzeller, Staffelkapitän 1./JG 54,
Schrunden/Courland, November 1944

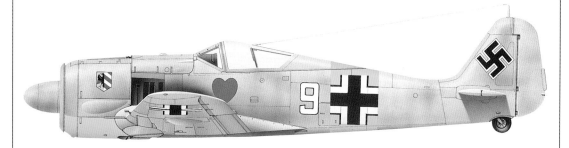

34
Fw 190A-4 'White 9', flown by Feldwebel Karl Schnörrer, 1./JG 54,
Krasnogvardeisk, circa January 1943

35
Fw 190A-4 'White 2', flown by Oberfeldwebel Anton Döbele, 1./JG 54,
Krasnogvardeisk, Spring 1943

36
Fw 190A-4 'White 3', flown by Feldwebel Peter Bremer, 1./JG 54,
Orel, July 1943

37
Fw 190A-4 'Black 5', flown by Hauptmann Hans Götz, Staffelkapitän 2./JG 54,
circa July 1943

38
Fw 190A-4 'Black 11', flown by Feldwebel Hans-Joachim Kroschinski, 2./JG 54,
Krasnogvardeisk, February 1943

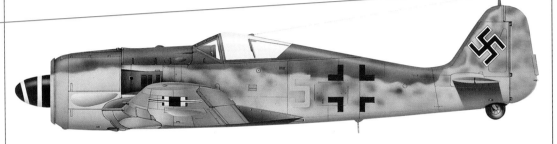

39
Fw 190A-6 'Yellow 5', flown by Oberleutnant Otto Kittel, 3./JG 54,
Riga-Skulte, circa August 1944

40
Fw 190A-5 'Yellow 8', flown by Leutnant Robert Weiss, 3./JG 54,
Orel, circa June 1943

41
Fw 190A-6 'Black Double Chevron', flown by Major Erich Rudorffer, Gruppenkommandeur II./JG 54,
Immola/Finland, June 1944

42
Fw 190A-6 'Black 5', flown by Oberleutnant Max Stotz, 5./JG 54,
Siverskaya, late Spring 1943

43
Fw 190A-6 'Black 7', flown by Leutnant Emil Lang, 5./JG 54,
Northern Sector, Summer 1943

44
Fw 190A-4 'Black 12', flown by Fähnrich Norbert Hannig, 5/JG 54,
Siverskaya, circa May 1943

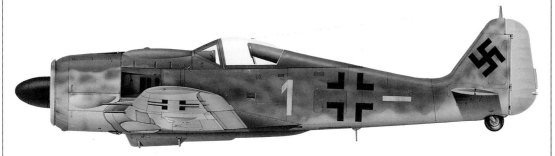

45
Fw 190A-4 'Yellow 6', flown by Oberleutnant Hans Beisswenger, Staffelkapitän 6./JG 54,
Ryelbitzi, February 1943

46
Fw 190A-9 'Yellow 1', flown by Hauptmann Helmut Wettstein, Staffelkapitän 6./JG 54,
Libau-Grobin/Courland, February 1945

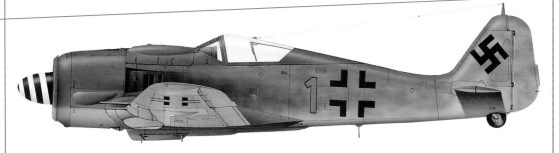

47
Fw 190A-8 'Yellow 1', flown by Leutnant Gerd Thyben, Staffelkapitän 7./JG 54,
Libau-Grobin/Courland, circa January 1945

48
Fw 190A-4 'Yellow 2', flown by Oberfeldwebel Heinrich Sterr, 6./JG 74, circa March 1943

49
Fw 190A-8 'White 3', flown by Oberleutnant Karl Brill, Staffelkapitän 10./JG 54,
Lemberg (Lwow)/Poland, summer 1944

50
Fw 190F-2 'Black Chevron and Bars', flown by Major Alfred Druschel, Geschwaderkommodore, Schl.G 1,
Varvarovka, Summer 1943

51
Fw 190F-2 'Black Double Chevron', flown by Hauptmann Georg Dörffel, Gruppenkommandeur I/Schl.G 1,
Kharkov, circa February 1943

52
Fw 190F-2 'Black Chevron', flown by Oberleutnant Karl Kennel, Staffelkapitän 5./Schl.G 1,
Varvarovka, July 1943

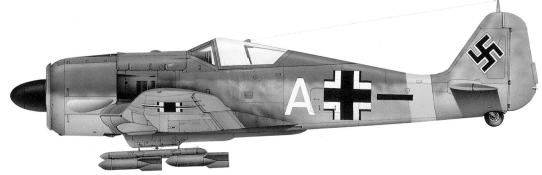

53
Fw 190F-2 'White A', flown by Leutnant Fritz Seyffardt, 6./Schl.G 1,
Ukraine, circa May 1943

54
Fw 190F-2 'Black T', flown by Oberfeldwebel Otto Dommeratzky, 8./Schl.G 1,
Southern Sector, September 1943

55
Fw 190D-9 'Black Chevron and Bars', flown by Oberst Hans-Ulrich Rudel, Gesch
waderkommodore SG2, Grossenhain, April 1945

56
Fw 190F-2 'Black Double Chevron', flown by Major Heinz Frank, Gruppenkommandeur II./SG 2,
Karankut/Crimea, April 1944

57
Fw 190F-9 'Black Double Chevron/2', flown by Major Karl Kennel, Gruppenkommandeur II./SG 2,
Börgönd/Hungary, circa December 1944

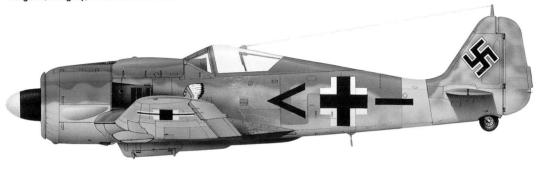

58
Fw 190F-8 'Black Chevron', flown by Leutnant Hermann Buchner, Staffelkapitän 4./SG 2,
Zilistea/Rumania, June 1944

59
Fw 190A-5 'Black G', flown by Oberfeldwebel August Lambert, 5./SG 2,
Southern Sector, late 1943

60
Fw 190F-8 'Black Chevron/Green H' flown by Hauptmann Günther Bleckmann, Staffelkapitän 6./SG 2,
Bacau/Rumania, May 1944

1
3./JG 54's Oberfeldwebel Otto Kittel, the top scoring Fw 190 pilot on the Eastern Front, in early 1944

2
The highest scoring *Schlachtflieger* of them all, Leutnant August Lambert of 5./SG 2 in early 1944

3
Long-time *Kommodore* of JG 54, Oberstleutnant Hannes Trautloft as he appeared in autumn 1943

4
Oberfeldwebel Hermann Buchner of
4./SG 2 is seen in his lightweight
summer kit in spring 1944

5
The most famous Fw 190 pilot of
them all, Walter Nowotny runs for
his Fw 190 in October 1943

6
Oberleutnant Joachim Brendel, a
189-victory ace with JG 51, is seen
between sorties in the spring of 1944

JG 51 REVERTS TO TYPE . . .

For JG 51 the writing was plainly on the wall with the conversion of its IV. *Gruppe* back on to the Bf 109 in the immediate aftermath of Kursk. And the events which were to follow did little to ease the supply situation regarding replacement aircraft for the *Geschwader*'s two remaining Fw 190 *Gruppen*. Forced to vacate Orel post-haste in the face of the advancing Soviets, I. and III./JG 51 retired first to the even greater confusion and gross overcrowding of Bryansk. They did not stay there long, however. Major Erich Leie's *Gruppe* was soon despatched southwards, to the Poltava area, to help stem the developing Russian threat against Kharkov. III./JG 51, under Hauptmann Fritz Losigkeit, were initially sent north-westwards to bar Smolensk to the enemy. But when the Red Army opened another offensive, this time aimed at Kiev, III. *Gruppe* also suddenly found themselves en route to the Ukraine.

This war of movement, and of subsequent continual retreat, set the pattern for the remainder of 1943. It was to prove costly in aircraft as the accident rate climbed and machines under repair had to be either abandoned or blown up before each hasty retirement. By the end of August the two *Gruppen* were each down to half strength or less. They would rarely be able to improve upon this state of affairs in the months ahead.

But despite all the difficulties, scores continued to mount. Collectively, JG 51 had claimed its 5000th kill on 2 June. By 15 September this figure had risen to 7000. Another 1000 would be added by the end of April 1944. Individually, a number of *Experten* topped the 100 mark during this period. *Gruppenkommandeur* Major Erich Leie – 'Tiger-Leie' – got his hundredth on 11 November. Oberleutnant Joachim 'Achim' Brendel, a long-serving member of Leie's *Gruppe*, followed suit just 11 days later. In III./JG 51 two future *Staffelkapitäne* were particularly successful. Oberleutnant Karl-Heinz Weber had achieved his century on 13 August. In the course of that same month Leutnant Günther Schack had added 40 kills to his score before reaching his hundredth on 3 September.

Extracts from Günther Schack's reports of the time offer an insight into the chaotic nature of that late summer and early autumn:

'7 August: We transfer to a little field east of Smolensk.

'8 August: The balloon goes up at 16.00 hours. We escort bombers to Yelnya. In the late afternoon the entire *Gruppe* scrambles (each *Staffel* has no more than four machines). Low-flying Russian aircraft are reported at Yarzevo. I am the first to reach them. Sitting ducks, so I am able to waggle my wings twice as I land back at base. My *Rotte* is ordered to take off again immediately without waiting to refuel or rearm. We are to escort another bomber unit. At 16,000 ft over the target two enemy fighters attack. One soon goes down in flames near the bombers; the other quickly makes off. On the third sortie we meet 25 '*Zementers*' escorted by 40 fighters. As there are only the two of us I climb up to the highest ones and manage to shoot two down. Every day we have to fight against an enemy who enjoys a numerical superiority such as we have never experienced in Russia before; large squadrons of bombers escorted by many fighters."

The following day Schack scored his 70th kill, his Fw190 being damaged in return by two cannon and two machine-gun hits. Four days after that he completed his 500th sortie, scored four kills in the course of it, and brought his total to 75. On 15 August Schack had a close call when, together with two young pilots of 9. *Staffel*, he was escorting Ju 87s. Due to a faulty gunsight he took longer than usual to despatch a Soviet fighter. As his two companions were no longer in view, he had no witnesses to his victory. Spotting a flak battery near the crash site, he dived down rocking his wings and inviting the gun crews to confirm his kill. Their reply was a fusilade of shells. The latest intelligence reports were already out of date; the area was in Russian hands!

With a hole of about 20 inches diameter in his port wing, Schack had difficulty in controlling his aircraft. But by pressing his knee against the control column he was able to maintain level flight, slowly climb from the 300 ft altitude at which he had been hit, and safely make it back to base.

For the next three days the *Staffel* was unable to fly any missions at all as it did not have a single aircraft serviceable. Shortly afterwards they moved the short distance to Bryansk, where they joined forces with II./JG 54 down from the north, before both were transferred to the Ukraine.

On 27 August, again accompanied by two other pilots, Schack engaged a large bomber formation escorted by about 30 fighters. He managed to bring down one bomber (his 90th kill), but then the three Fw 190s were set upon by the escorts, and had great difficulty in extricating themselves.

Another sortie later that same day was again very nearly his last. While attacking a Soviet fighter, Schack was accidentally rammed by Oberfeld-webel Lothar Mai, an *Experte* with 45 kills, who was apparently so intent upon attacking the same fighter that he did not see Schack. Mai's 190 went straight in from about 12,000 ft, crashing alongside the Russian. There was no sign of a parachute from either machine. Luckily, Schack managed to pull his damaged Fw 190 out of its spin and limp home.

Two days later, the *Staffel* moved to Konotop. On 1 September the *Gruppe* scored a total of 40 victories, but Schack was forced to belly-land after each of the four missions he flew that day. Forty-eight hours later he achieved his 100th kill. *Gruppenkommandeur* Hauptmann Fritz Losigkeit was also in the air at the time:

'Günther from *Hannibal,* congratulations on the 100th!'

Shortly afterwards III./JG 51 was ordered back to the Bryansk area. On 12 September another move took them to Rosslavl. Three days later – the day the *Geschwader* recorded its 7000th victory – their destination was Smolensk. On 19 September they transferred to Mogilev. By 10 October they were at Vitebsk. And so it went on. From one field to the next. But all the time being pushed slowly backwards. Under conditions such as these, it is little wonder that they were suffering a lengthening list of casualties, which was now beginning to include a growing toll of young replacement pilots who were falling victim to the Soviet's overwhelming superiority in numbers before they themselves had been able to achieve a single kill.

But, in the end, it was the availability, or, rather, the non-availability, of Fw 190s which dictated the future for JG 51. Focke-Wulf's production line simply could not keep pace with demand; demand not only from the Home and Western Fronts, but now also for specialized ground-attack variants. Early in 1944 I./JG 51 began withdrawing to Deblin-Irena for re-equipment with the Bf 109G. When they returned to Bobruisk on the Central Sector in March, it was the turn of III. *Gruppe* to retire to Deblin for similar conversion. Thus, by the beginning of May, all three Eastern Front *Gruppen* of JG 51 were mounted on the Bf 109G. They would fly the 'Gustav' for the final 12 months of the war.

There was, however, one small link in the chain between JG 51 and the Fw 190 which remained unbroken throughout. When II./JG 51 had been forced to abandon its conversion programme on to the Fw 190 after news of the Anglo-American landings in north-west Africa late in 1942, only two of its component *Staffeln*, 4. and 5./JG 51, had been sent to the Mediterranean. Oberleutnant Diethelm von Eichel-Streiber's 6./JG 51 had stayed on at Jesau to complete re-equipment with the Fw 190 before returning to the Eastern Front in the company of III. *Gruppe*. Shortly after their arrival back in Russia, 6./JG 51 had been redesignated as the *Stabsstaffel* (HQ squadron), being used thereafter on a semi-autonomous basis either to bolster the strength of the regular four-aircraft *Stabss-chwarm*, or to be otherwise deployed under the direct control of the *Geschwaderkommodore*. Its average strength numbering about a dozen aircraft during the whole of its two-and-a-half-year history, the *Stabsstaffel* flew the Fw 190 from beginning to end, although sometimes operating a handful of Bf 109s as well. Hauptmann von Eichel-Streiber remained at its head until the close of April 1944, when he replaced Fritz Losigkeit as *Kommandeur* of III./JG 51 (the latter having been promoted to *Geschwaderkommodore*). During his tenure of command of the *Stabsstaffel* von Eichel-Streiber had added some 70 kills to the 5 he had scored while serving with previous units. He ended the war as a member of JV 44 flying the Me 262 and with a final total of 96 victories, all but two of which had been achieved on the Eastern Front.

Von Eichel-Streiber's immediate successors were neither as long-serving, nor as fortunate. *Staffelkapitän* Hauptmann Edwin Thiel succumbed to Soviet flak over Kobryn in Poland on 14 July 1944 with his score standing at 76. The *Stabsstaffel* lost four pilots the following month, including Oberfeldwebel Fritz Lüddecke, a 50-victory *Experte* who also fell victim to enemy anti-aircraft fire, this time near Wilkowischken (Vilkaviskis) on the Lithuanian border close to East Prussia on 10 August, and Oberleutnant Heinz Busse, the *Stabsstaffel's* third *Kapitän*, who had a total of 22 kills to his credit when he was shot down in a dogfight over the same area 15 days later.

The mention above of East Prussia indicates just how far JG 51 had been forced to retreat during 1944. From Bobruisk on the River Beresina in the spring, the *Stabsstaffel* had withdrawn, via Terespol, to Memel on the Baltic coast by September, and thence back across the borders of the *Reich* itself from Insterburg in central East Prussia to Neukuhren, once more on the shores of the Baltic, by the year's end. Here, five months later, the *Mölders Geschwader*, including the *Stabsstaffel*, would make its last stand.

. . . BUT THE 'GREEN HEARTS' SOLDIER ON

The series of powerful Soviet counter-strokes which followed on from Kursk were all targeted across the Central and Southern Sectors. Throughout 1943 the Northern Sector, locked solid around the continuing siege of Leningrad, remained relatively stable (there were 12 Russian armies deployed along the front north of Velikiye Luki compared with 49 to the south) and curiously detached from the maelstrom that had been unleashed below.

But for JG 54's two Fw 190 *Gruppen* the settled, almost comfortable, lifestyle enjoyed at Krasnogvardeisk and Siverskaya would soon become but a dim memory. I./JG 54 had already had a foretaste of what was to come. Their transfer south to back up JG 51 in the opening rounds of *Zitadelle* early in July had cost them three leaders – Seiler, Homuth and Götz – in very short order. In August I. *Gruppe*, under the caretaker command of Oberleutnant Otto Vincent, was joined on the Central Sector by detachments from both II./JG 54 and the newly activated, Bf 109-equipped IV. *Gruppe*. They too now became part of the hopelessly outnumbered 'fire brigade', shuttling between *Luftflotte* 6 and *Luftflotte* 4, as the Red Army bore down on the defenders of the central front and threatened to engulf the Ukraine. It was during the turmoil of the closing months of 1943 that one man was to soar to prominence; arguably to become the most famous Eastern Front Fw 190 *Experte* of them all.

In August Oberleutnant Walter Nowotny added 49 kills to his score (a total, coincidentally, matched exactly by JG 52's rising star Erich Hartmann to the south – Hartmann would claim his century on 20 September, Nowotny's hundredth had gone down on 15 June). On 21 August Walter Nowotny was promoted from *Staffelkapitän* of 1./JG 54 to the command of I. *Gruppe*. His reaction in a letter home was typical:

'Got my 161st yesterday, in other words 37 in 10 days. Also informed I was to be the new *Kommandeur*. Two happy events that we celebrated accordingly! It's not every day that a 22^1/$_2$-year-old Oberleutnant gets made up to *Kommandeur*; that's normally a Major's post, which means that sooner or later I'll get to be a Hauptmann or perhaps even a Major. Something I'd never dreamed of. Still no sign of the Oak Leaves though.'

Nowotny was obviously displaying early symptoms of 'throat-ache', Luftwaffe slang for those who were eager to receive some new decoration to hang around their necks. His mystification was understandable. The Oak Leaves to his Knight's Cross were certainly long overdue. In the first year of the war about 40 victories would have assured a fighter pilot of the coveted Oak Leaves. By 1941-42 this figure had risen to nearer the 100 mark. Now, in 1943, some 120 kills were required before the 'Cauliflower', as the award was known by the more irreverent, could be anticipated. And Nowotny had gained his 120th back on 24 June; one of ten Russian aircraft he had shot down that day.

Despite the apparent lack of official appreciation, Nowotny went from strength to strength. He had around him three inseparable companions: his *Katschmarek*, Karl 'Quax' Schnörrer (whose unusual nickname derived from a popular film of the period chronicling the misadventures of an accident-prone pilot), Anton 'Toni' Döbele and Rudolf Rademacher. This team, the Nowotny-*Schwarm*, became justly famous – between them they accounted for 524 enemy aircraft destroyed!

On 1 September Nowotny claimed another ten kills; seven in the space of 17 minutes during a morning sortie and three within nine minutes after lunch. Part of his description of the day's events reads:

'At 06.00 hours we were escorting bombers at high altitude when we were approached by six Soviet fighters. I managed to bring down four of them. Then I saw another five circling below us. I got two of these and was after the third when my cannon jammed. "*Teufel*", I thought to myself, "this would have to happen 180 kilometres behind the enemy lines. (Nowotny was obviously no proponent of remaining within safe gliding distance of friendly territory!). But I was determined to get that seventh one, and so I gave chase, closing right up on him to let him have it with my machine-guns. By the time he'd finally bought it, we were right over a large town, bang in the middle of a barrage of 20 mm flak. Nothing for it but to dive down to street level. At a height of five metres I followed the roads out, hopping over flak enplacements and houses, before escaping by climbing over a patch of open, swampy ground on the edge of town.

'In the afternoon we bumped into just five Soviet fighters. When things got too hot for them, they began playing hide-and-seek in the cumulus clouds. But I waited around until one or the other poked his nose out. This happened three times, and made it a total of ten for the day."

It was at this time, shortly before his 190th victory, that Nowotny's brother wrote him a letter. In it he pointed out that people such as Mölders, Galland and Marseille had achieved nothing like the same number of kills as he had, and yet they had all received the Diamonds to their Knight's Cross. Had Walter said or done something to upset the powers-that-be? Nowotny's reply, scribbled on a postcard from the front, was brief and to the point:

'In answer to your last letter:

1. None of your business.

2. Why are you worrying your head about my problems?

3. If they don't want to give me the Oak Leaves, I'll get myself the Diamonds.

Yours, Walter.'

And he proceeded to do just that!

On 4 September 1943 Oberleutnant Walter Nowotny finally became the 293rd member of the Wehrmacht (German Armed Forces) to be awarded the Oak Leaves to the Knight's Cross. There had been nothing sinister about the delay; the stakes had simply been upped another 70 or so since the 120 kills needed earlier in the year, and Nowotny just happened to be the first recipient to have to meet the new criteria! But someone in authority must have taken note of the apparent injustice. For when, less than three weeks later, he was summoned to Hitler's HQ to be presented with his Oak Leaves, he had already been awarded the next highest order, the Swords, as well. On 22 September, looking suitably dignified, Nowotny lined up with other fighter and night-fighter aces to receive his decorations from the hands of the *Führer* himself. Back at *Gruppe* the mood was less formal. Toasts were drunk to the 'Old Man's' getting the double: The 'Cauliflower' *and* the 'Knife and Fork'!

In those intervening 17 days Nowotny's total had risen by another 29. It made him the Luftwaffe's top scorer of the time. A war correspondent was on hand to record the events:

'For two days nothing had happened. With 203 enemy aircraft destroyed the *Kommandeur* was among the leading ranks of successful fighter pilots. But could he get just those few extra to put him ahead of all the others? It was cool, clear weather with perfect visibility; but not a Bolshevik to be seen in the sky. Then, about midday on 14 September the sound of flak. A large formation of enemy bombers, strongly escorted by fighters, was approaching the base.

'Our fighters scrambled – but without their *Kommandeur*. He was away on a Stuka-escort mission. On his return he immediately led his *Schwarm* off on a *Freie Jagd* sweep. Soon, the one word everybody in the ops room had been waiting to hear. "*Aufpassen*" ("Watch out"); the *Kommandeurs*'s voice over the loudspeaker. It was the word he used every time he scored a kill, requesting his *Katschmarek* to observe and confirm the victory. Oberleutnant Nowotny had his 204th. Soon after he added the 205th, 206th, 207th . . .

'Oberleutnant Walter Nowotny had just become the Luftwaffe's most successful fighter pilot. But when he lands there is no time for congratulations. The Bolsheviks seem to be softening the ground for a new breakthough with massive air attacks. The *Kommandeur* changes machines and takes to the air again.'

Major von Bonin, *Geschwaderkommodore* of JG 54, on the left, discusses the Berlin awards ceremony with Hauptmann Walter Nowotny shortly after the latter's return with both the Oak Leaves and Swords

Within days of returning from the *Führer* HQ, Nowotny, now promoted to Hauptmann, had taken his score to 235. Oberleutnant Hübner, the war correspondent again:

'Yesterday evening the *Kommandeur* suddenly arrived back. Nobody was expecting him. After the awards ceremony he had been due a long spell of home leave. But, he said, he'd spent two enjoyable days in Vienna and that was enough.

'After many miserable and overcast days, this morning it is perfect autumnal weather, clear and fresh. The best uniform is packed away and the old Russian front flying gear is put back on, including the famous "victory trousers". These show several large repairs, and are turning grey from age and constant use. But the *Kommandeur* won't be parted from them, even if they are just about ready for the museum.'

The skies south of Velikiye Luki were alive with enemy air activity. That afternoon Nowotny shot down three out of a gaggle of 14 Airacobras which he had spotted some 1000 metres below on an opposing course. The first went down in steep spirals, leaving a corkscrew trail of smoke which hung for some minutes in the still air to mark the spot. The second exploded, followed by the third only moments later. 'Quax' Schnörrer claimed a fourth.

The next day was a replay of the last. The six Airacobras they encountered may even have been survivors from the previous afternoon, for no sooner had they sighted the Focke-Wulfs than they turned tail and fled back eastwards. Only two made it. The following day was a write-off. Nowotny's guns jammed in the middle of a dogfight. And when he got back to base his only other machine was unserviceable.

Twenty-four hours later he had more success. Four enemy machines downed in the space of nine minutes: a Curtiss P-40, an Airacobra, a LaGG-3 and another P-40. The latter was number 235.

It took almost a month to rack up the next 15. On 9 October Nowotny himself scored JG 54's 6000th victory of the war. Then, four days later, as Oberleutnant Hübner recounts:

'Just as our Ju 87s went into the attack they were set upon by enemy fighters. Nowotny managed to shoot a P-40 off the tail of a diving Stuka. The Russian hit the ground and was engulfed in the explosions of the Junker's bombs. Climbing to engage another Bolshevik, Nowotny was unaware that a P-40 was on his own tail until a warning shout from his *Katschmarek*. The odds were with the attacker, but Nowotny managed to out-turn him and bring him down.

'The Stukas had departed by now, but the Hauptmann hung back and was rewarded by the sight of several more enemy fighters flitting low over the frontlines. One diving pass gained him his 246th.

'The next day several Bolshevik fighters tried to prevent one of our reconnaissance machines from carrying out its task. Nowotny disposed of three of them and suddenly the others were nowhere to be seen. The reconnaissance aircraft had a clear run.

'Finally, combing the frontline area one last time, he discovered a single enemy fighter, a P-40. It proved to be a worthy opponent. The dogfight lasted some ten minutes before the Curtiss finally crashed to the ground. Number 250!

'Wild celebrations back at base. The commander of the field's flak defences sent up a victory salute and there was a veritable firework display of flares to greet the returning flyer, the first fighter pilot in the world to score 250 kills.'

There was a postscript, too. After receiving a telephone call from General Ritter von Greim, C-in-C *Luftflotte* 6, who was the first to offer official congratulations, Nowotny took Schnörrer to one side:

'"Quax", I promised myself that if I ever got my 250th I'd really celebrate. I'm going to take the courier aircraft to Vilna and really tie one on. Why don't you come with me?'

Schnörrer regretfully declined. Somebody had to stay behind and mind the shop. So Nowotny took the *Gruppe*'s MO with him in the Bf 108 to Vilna, leaving Schnörrer to organise the base festivities. As these included emptying the mess of its entire stock of wines and spirits – at Nowotny's express invitation and expense – it was not long before everybody was more than a little merry.

And it was at this point in the proceedings that another call from 'Papa' Greim came through. Nowotny was wanted on the phone again. 'Quax' Schnörrer:

'Everybody looked in my direction. I shook myself and tried to stand up, hot and cold at the same time. I knew where Nowotny was to be found. But how could I explain this to the General?

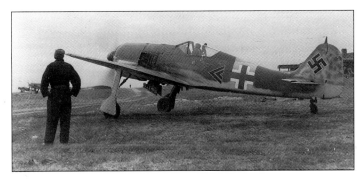

'I slumped against the phone and tried to clear my throat. All I could get out was a hoarse "*Herr General*". Hardly had I spoken when the General cut in, "You old *Wildsau*. You're drunk, aren't you?"

'There was no point denying it, "*Jawohl*."

'"Papa" Greim was an old World War 1 flyer and understood the situation perfectly. "For God's sake, 'Quax'", he bellowed, "pull yourself together and tell me where Nowotny's hiding himself. The *Führer* wants to congratulate him and give him the Diamonds."

'I was sober in an instant, "*Herr General*, Nowotny's in the Ria-Bar in Vilna. He's having a party."

'"So that's it. Well, the signals people are really going to have to show us what they can do. You be ready at 08.00 hours too, you're accompanying 'Nowy' to the *Führer*."

'I put the phone down and hurried back into the mess. Despite my "acting *Kommandeur*ship", I had a hard time calling for peace and quiet amidst the general uproar. When I repeated my phone conversation with "Papa" Greim the noise and jubilation, if anything, grew even louder. But a few older and wiser heads began to worry about the outcome. The signals staff would never manage to connect Hitler with the Ria-Bar, they prophesied. And what then?

'But in the event they did. "Nowy" described to me later how he was called to the phone. He heard the voice of an adjutant, "I'm connecting you to the *Führer*." "Nowy" nearly fell through the floor. There he was, propped up on a bar stool in Lithuania, surrounded by a bevy of young ladies, listening, between the hubbub, to the voice of the Commander-in-Chief of the German Armed Forces calling in person from his headquarters in East Prussia to inform him that he had just been awarded the Reich's highest military decoration!

'"Had Adolf known where I really was, I reckon he would have had second thoughts about the Diamonds", 'Nowy' confessed.

'Next morning General von Greim's He 111 arrived at Vitebsk to collect me. We flew to Vilna to pick "Nowy" up and we both had a quick bath and changed into our best uniforms before the flight to East Prussia. There we were met by a huge Mercedes and driven to the *Führer's* HQ through three sets of checkpoints. We were offered coffee and sandwiches, but our heads were still spinning from the night before. My face was as white as cheese, and I felt as if I would rather die than stand to attention in front of Hitler. So it was agreed that I would wait outside with the adjutant while "Nowy" went into the inner sanctum alone.

'He came out about an hour later with a broad smile on his face. The

Fw 190A-6 Werk-Nr 410004 was the aircraft with which Hauptmann Nowotny scored his 250th kill. This event took place on 14 October 1943, and his victim was a skillfully flown lend-lease P-40 – the dogfight involving the two protagonists lasted a full 10 minutes! Part of I./JG 54, this aircraft is seen being taxied out from its dispersal at Vitebsk in November 1943

This official portrait was taken soon after Nowotny had been awarded the Diamonds by the *Führer* in Berlin. The award is clearly visible, along with the Knight's Cross, Oak Leaves and Swords at his throat

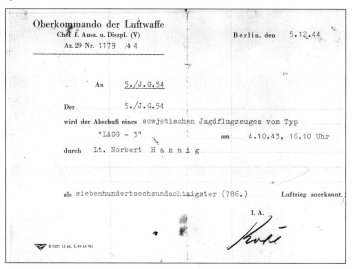

A LaGG-3 downed by Leutnant Norbert Hannig on 4 October 1943 gave 5.*Staffel* its 786th kill of the war, but just look at how long it has taken official confirmation to come through from the *OKL* – the date on the document, top right, reads 5.12.1944!

'Bully' Lang's 18 kills in one day got him on the cover of the 13 January 1944 issue of Berlin's fortnightly *Illustrierte* magazine. The headline at the foot of the cover reads 'Eighteen in one day: the victor returns'. Lang, of II./JG 54, scored this world record tally in late October 1943 near Kiev

Diamonds sparkled at his neck. As we left, Hilter was standing outside his bunker, lost in thought and holding "Blondi" his German shepherd on her lead. In passing, Nowotny could not resist the temptation of formally introducing me to the *Führer*!'

Meanwhile, the daily life-or-death struggles along the front continued unabated. Successes such as Nowotny's, and one or two other stellar individuals' – like Leutnant Emil 'Bully' Lang, II. *Gruppe*'s one-time unsuccessful popper of rivets, who achieved the world's all-time record of 18 kills in one day over the Kiev region late in October – had to be measured against a growing rate of attrition. Shuttling between three *Luftflotten*, from Leningrad to the Ukraine, JG 54 lost some 30 pilots during the final months of 1943. And although many of the casualties were untried youngsters, the ranks of the experienced '*Alte Hasen*' were inevitably thinning too.

On 11 October the famous 'Nowotny *Schwarm*' was finally broken up by the loss of Leutnant Anton Döbele, who was killed in a mid-air collision with another German fighter over the Smolensk-Vitebsk supply highway. 'Toni' Döbele's score stood just four short of the 100. His death marked the end of an era. The following day 'Quax' Schnörrer was seriously injured. He and Nowotny had scrambled in pouring rain to answer calls for help from infantry under attack by *Stormoviks* near Nevel. Despite the appalling visibility they had each managed to down one of the Russians before Nowotny suddenly shouted:

'Quax, break left, you're burning!'

The fire spread rapidly. 'Bale out, you'll never land in those trees!' Nowotny watched as his *Katschmarek* tried to extricate himself from the flames licking around the cockpit. Just below cloud level, only some 50-70 metres from the ground, he finally succeeded. His auxiliary chute had only just begun to deploy the main canopy when 'Quax' disappeared into the muck below. Despite concussion and two broken legs, Schnörrer was rescued from the woods by the infantrymen and collected by Nowotny in a Fieseler Storch. He recovered after a long stay in hospital and returned to operations on Me 262s towards the end of the war. During his service with JG 54 Leutnant Karl Schnörrer, primary guardian of Nowotny's tail, had himself claimed 35 kills.

It was on 15 November 1943 that Nowotny scored his own 255th and last Eastern Front victory. He was later posted as *Kommodore* to a training *Geschwader* before assuming command of the Me 262 test unit which bore his name. The exact sequence of events surrounding the air battle and subsequent crash which led to his death at Achmer on 8 November 1944 has never been fully ascertained.

The 'Green Hearts' lost only one of their *Kommodore* in action. This was on 15 December when Oberstleutnant Hubertus von Bonin was shot down near Vitebsk. Von Bonin, who had taken over from Oberst Trautloft in July, had achieved 77 victories, including four while serving with the 'Condor Legion' in Spain. His replacement at the head of JG 54 was Major Mader, previously *Kommodore* of JG 11 in the west.

In mid-January 1944 the North Sector of the front, so long dormant, suddenly exploded into life with the launching of a major Red Army offensive. The capture of Mga on 21 January heralded the lifting of the almost 900-day siege of Leningrad. I. and II./JG 54 were hurriedly recalled from the Central and Southern Sectors respectively. Returning to their old stamping grounds, it quickly became clear that this new northern tide of the Russian advance would prove as impossible to stem as that currently surging across the Ukraine far to the south. In fact, JG 54 soon found themselves retracing their steps back through the Baltic States almost as rapidly as their predecessors had advanced across them during that balmy summer of 1941.

By February I. *Gruppe*, commanded since Nowotny's departure by Hauptmann Horst Ademeit, had taken up residence at Wesenberg in Estonia. They were joined the following month by II./JG 54, who occupied Dorpat and Petschur (Petseri) west of Lakes Peipus and Pleskau. Fortunately it was a time of minimal losses for the two Fw 190 *Gruppen*. Successes continued to mount, however, and on 23 March, with his 135th kill, Leutnant Albin Wolf scored the *Geschwader*'s 7000th victory. *Staffelkapitän* of 6./JG 54 since Ademeit's promotion, Wolf was killed by a direct flak hit over Pleskau ten days later. In those ten days he had downed another nine enemy aircraft, bringing his final total to 144; no mean feat for a pilot who had once described the Fw 190 as 'landing like a wet sack!'

In June 1944 the Soviets unleashed their massive Central Front summer offensive which would cut off the coastal regions of the Baltic States to the north from the main bodies of the German armies being pushed back towards the borders of the Reich. At the same time the Russians attacked the Finnish forces still occupying the Karelian Isthmus north of Leningrad. In the face of the former threat, I./JG 54 vacated Estonia for neighbouring Latvia, first detaching 1. *Staffel* briefly to Turku in Finland to protect German naval units in the northern Baltic. In response to the latter, Major Erich Rudorffer's II. *Gruppe* also went to Finland as the fighter component of *Gefechtsverband* (Battle Group) Kuhlmey, a mixed-bag formation of Stukas and ground-attack Fw 190s sent to aid the hard-pressed Finns. During their month's sojourn at Immola in northern Karelia II./JG 54 claimed 66 Soviet aircraft destroyed.

A surprise arrival on the Russian Front that same June was a rejuvenated and reinforced IV./JG 54. After earlier retiring through Rumania, this Bf 109 *Gruppe* had withdrawn to Germany to re-equip with Fw 190A-8s and be brought up to full current Defence of the Reich

Geschwaderkommodore **Hubertus von Bonin (left) was shot down and killed near JG 54's base at Vitebsk on 15 December 1943. He scored 77 kills, including four in Spain as part of the 'Condor Legion'**

144-victory ace Oberfeldwebel Albin Wolf gets JG 54's 7000th victory of the war on 23 March 1944. A motley looking group of 'black men' look on with weary approval

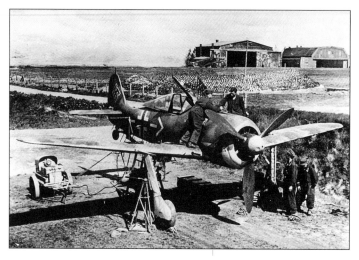

The *Geschwaderkommodore's* machine undergoes gun calibration following routine servicing away from the frontline at Dorpat, in Estonia, on 18 July 1944. Major Anton Mader's Fw 190A-6 wears a white command chevron and bars, as per regulations. The scheme worn by the A-6 is typical of that adopted by the recce assets of *Luftflotte* 1 in the northern sector of the front, and consisted of an upper surface camouflage pattern of green and brown

Rushed to the Finnish front in June 1944 to protect German naval units in the northern Baltic, 'White 4' of 4.*Staffel* II./JG 54 is seen at Immola during a lull between sorties. It has its upper engine inspection panel hinged open, which may mean that the machine has been temporily grounded with a technical write up. Also suffering engine problems in the background is a Finnish Air Force Brewster Buffalo

establishment of four *Staffeln* each of 16 aircraft. In one of the first instances of precedence being given to the Eastern Front over home defence requirements, IV./JG 54 was suddenly despatched to the Soviet-Polish border region on 30 June to provide air cover for the retreating ground troops. Commanded by Major Wolfgang Späte - later to achieve fame as the *Kommodore* of JG 400, the rocket-powered Me 163 Komet unit – IV./JG 54 suffered grievously in the ensuing two months before retiring back to the Reich early in September.

By that time the two long-serving Fw 190 *Gruppen*, I. and II./JG 54, had retired deeper into isolated Latvia, occupying bases on the Courland peninsula at Schrunden (Cirava) and Libau-Grobin respectively. It was during this period, too, that a final round of personnel and organisational changes took place. On 8 August Major Horst Ademeit had been reported missing in action. A rare occurrence, his Fw 190 had succumbed to infantry fire over Dünaburg in southernmost Latvia and was last seen going down behind enemy lines. A member of JG 54 since the days of the Battle of Britain, Ademeit's score was standing at 166 at the time of his disappearance. His place at the head of I. *Gruppe* was filled by Major Franz Eisenach, who had served as *Staffelkapitän* of 3./JG 54 before being severely wounded back in May 1943.

And at the end of September Oberstleutnant Mader relinquished command of the *Geschwader* to Oberst Dietrich Hrabak. A highly experienced *Kommodore*, late of JG 52, Hrabak's career had begun as far back as February 1938. He too had flown with the 'Green Hearts' in the Battle of Britain and had been *Kommandeur* of II./JG 54 during the latter half of that conflict. The *Geschwader* could want for no better leader in the difficult days that lay ahead.

With all but the *Stabsstaffel* of JG 51 having converted back on to the Bf 109 in May, JG 54's two *Gruppen* were now effectively the sole Fw 190 fighter presence on the Eastern Front – albeit already bottled up in Courland. They also now underwent Defence of the Reich style reorganization, a fourth *Staffel* being added to each *Gruppe*. In theory, this translated into an official total establishment of well over 130 aircraft. The reality – as of mid-October – was that they could muster just 56 serviceable aircraft between them. And a new spectre was also beginning to make itself felt: the increasing scarcity of aviation fuel. With everything having to be ferried in to

Courland by either air or sea, the fuel situation would soon reach crisis proportions. Before the end teams of oxen would be employed to move aircraft to and from dispersals to prevent unnecessary taxying!

There was, however, one shortage they were not suffering from: pilots. The earlier wartime system whereby a pilot, upon the successful completion of his formal training programme, would be posted to the subordinate *Ergänzungsgruppe* (replacement wing) of the particular frontline unit he was scheduled to join, had been abandoned in 1942. Instead of each *Jagdgeschwader*'s operating what was, in effect, its own personal OTU to prepare its newly assigned pilots for frontline combat, henceforth this task would be taken over by the official *Ergänzungsjagdgeschwader* (replacement fighter group), a unit intended to supply the entire fighter arm with combat-ready pilots.

This new EJG was divided into two *Gruppen*, '*Ost*' and '*West*', these in turn composed of a number of *Staffeln*, each of which was responsible for supplying the requirements of a particular *Jagdgeschwader*. Frontline pilots from these *Jagdgeschwader* were rotated back to their specific *Ergänzungsstaffel* to help prepare the trainees for the conditions they would face when posted forward to their operational unit.

JG 54's *Ergänzungsstaffel* had initially been based in southwestern France, at Bergerac, Biarritz and Toulouse, before retiring to the then greater safety of the Reich's eastern provinces, where they occupied Liegnitz, Rogau-Rosenau and Sagan. As with all training establishments, there were plenty of incidents. Some were tragic, like the pupil who tried a loop on his first flight and augered straight in from 2000 metres. Others less so. One hopeful, equipped with a belly tank, came in for a perfect three-pointer straight down the centre of the concrete runway, neglecting only to punch the button which lowered the undercarriage. As the first sparks began to fly, the onlookers closed their eyes and covered their ears . . . and nothing happened!

Another near textbook belly-landing was made by an instructor returning from an operational sortie - experienced *Ergänzungsstaffel* pilots often being called upon to participate in local air actions – when he realised that the starboard mainwheel indicator was not showing (this was a small metal rod which rose up out of the wing's top surface as the undercarriage

Above and below Problem rectified, 'White 4's' BMW awaits cranking up a session of post-rectification checks, prior to be leared for a return to the operations. Another Finnish Air Force stalwart fighter in the form of a Fiat G.50 is also out on the ramp at Immola undergoing power checks. II./JG 54 claimed 66 kills in just a month of operations from this northern Karelian base

leg was lowered). In the cockpit both green indicator lamps were on; but so were the reds. Better safe than sorry, he decided, and approached for a perfect wheels-up landing . . . with both legs locked securely down. Everybody in the *Staffel*, except him, had known that the right-hand indicator rod on this particular machine had been broken for days.

Although the basic training programmes were gradually curtailed as the war progressed (a result of the growing demand for quick replacements allied to declining fuel stocks), the *Ergänzungs* system continued. The frontline pilots did what they could with the ever more youthful and sketchily trained material passing through their hands. But the outcome was predictable. In the face of overwhelming enemy strength, many young pilots, however eager and willing, failed to return from their first mission.

Despite the official increase in complement, it also meant that there were more pilots available than there were machines to fly. This problem had plagued the Fw 190 *Gruppen* throughout their time on the Eastern Front, which is why few pilots, other than the higher ranking formation leaders, had individual aircraft permanently assigned to them. They were simply allocated a machine prior to a mission, the ground-crew adjusted the rudder pedals and seat height accordingly, and off they went.

On 16 October 1944 the Soviets launched their first attempt to destroy the Courland army. By March 1945 they would have mounted six separate offensives against the peninsula pocket. But the defenders resisted stubbornly. Hitler had expressly forbidden their evacuation. The *Führer* had a grandiose scheme of his own to use Courland as a springboard for a counterthrust southwards into the right flank of the main body of by-passing Russian armies. However, like many of his brainstorms in the last year of the war, this plan would come to nothing due to both a lack of men and machinery.

Unable to influence events elsewhere, the men of the Courland army simply clung on, fighting grimly for every inch of ground. And for the remaining six months of the war the task for each of I. and II./JG 54's 50-odd Fw 190s, whether flown by *Experte* or tyro, would be simply to protect them, and their vital sea and air supply routes, from the burgeoning 3600-plus fleet of aircraft on the combined Soviet Baltic and northern Belorussian fronts!

II./JG 54's young, yet seasoned, instructors take a break from the strenuous flying routine maintained seven days a week at Liegnitz, in Germany's eastern provinces, in the summer of 1944. Behind them are one of the many tented workshops quickly erected at the site following their recent move from more permanent locations in France. Many of these *Ergänzungsstaffel* pilots were called upon to fly hazardous local Defence of the Reich sorties when US bombers flew raids in their area

Enjoying a brief respite from the Russian Front, Leutnant Norbert Hannig is seen during his time as an instructor with *Ergänzungsgruppe Ost*, at Liegnitz, in June 1944

TOO LITTLE, TOO LATE

JG 54's enforced retirement into Baltic isolation meant that the *only* Fw 190s on the main Eastern fighting fronts during the latter half of 1944 were ground-attack machines. Despite a significant increase in numbers (the seven *Schlachtgruppen* of mid-1944 had grown to 12, plus several independent *Staffeln*, by the year's end), it was still a pitifully small force, some 300 serviceable aircraft in all, to place in the path of the greatest concentration of armour in military history as it erupted through the Vitebsk-Dnieper gap, the traditional 'gateway' for invading armies in, and out, of Russia.

Although their principal targets were the advancing Soviet ground forces, some *Schlacht* pilots still managed to add to their list of aerial kills. The heady days of the Crimea were long past, but II./SG 2, for example, tasked with flying escort for the Ju 87-equipped components of their parent *Geschwader* during the long retreat back across Rumania and Hungary, continued to take a steady toll of Russian fighters. Their success was not achieved without cost, however, one of the earliest victims of this final stage of the war having been Hauptmann Günther Bleckmann, *Staffelkapitän* of 6./SG 2, who had scored 27 kills before his death over Rumania on 4 June.

The following month Hauptmann Friedrich-Wilhelm Strakeljahn, who had led the ship-busting 14.(Jabo)/JG 5 to such effect over Arctic waters in 1943, and who had since returned to the Eastern Front as *Kommandeur* of II./SG 4, was downed by a direct flak hit near Macuty on the Northern Sector on 6 July.

In October Leutnant Otto Dommeratzky, also of 6./SG 2 and with close on 40 kills to his credit, lost his life in tragic circumstances when bounced by US fighters during an unarmed ferry flight over Czechoslovakia. With his crew chief – minus parachute – stowed uncom-

Seen in Rumania in July 1944, a I.*Gruppe Schlacht* Fw 190 sits quietly in the high grass as an impressive formation of five Bf 110s cruises past at low level. Note the tropical filter fitted to the F-8, which helped keep the sand and dust of the dry plains out of the BMW during taxying and take-off

A *Rotte* of II.*Gruppe* machines. Like the aircraft featured above, the wheel covers have been removed from these Fw 190F-8s – perhaps this signifies recent spring mud?

The greatest Stuka ace of them all. Major Hans-Ulrich Rudel's Ju 87s were often escorted by the Fw 190s of II./SG 2

A summer-uniformed Major Rudel being entertained in a unit mess. It is uncertain what's in the glass, as Rudel was a well-known teetotaller and keep-fit fanatic – a piece of Luftwaffe doggerel ran '*Major Rudel trinkt nur Sprudel*' (Major Rudel drinks only mineral water)

fortably in the fuselage behind him, Dommeratzky himself refused to bale out, electing instead to risk a crash-landing. Unfortunately he was unsuccessful and both were killed on impact.

The danger from American fighters was not new. P-51 Mustangs had first been encountered by II./SG 2 following their retreat from the Crimea into Rumania in June. A number of pilots, including two *Staffelkapitäne*, had already been lost to the Italian-based Americans. But as 1944 gave way to 1945 and the Germans were pushed steadily back – and the distance between their Eastern and Western Fronts diminished – so that danger grew. Marauding Allied fighters, rather than posing the occasional threat, bacame a constant menace. Nobody was safe. And on 17 April 1945 they claimed their greatest prize. Crimean ace Oberleutnant August Lambert, with 116 Russian aircraft destroyed, the highest scoring *Schlachtflieger* of them all and now *Staffelkapitän* of 8./SG 77, was taking off with his unit from Kamenz, northeast of Dresden, to attack the advancing Russians when he was jumped by 60 to 80 Mustangs. After a short but hopeless struggle he was brought down over Hoyerswerda some 12 miles away. Six other members of his *Staffel* died in the same sprawling, desperate dogfight.

To the north the RAF were proving equally predatory. On 30 April a group of Spitfires caught a formation of Fw 190s of I.(Pz)/SG 9, a specialised rocket-armed anti-tank *Gruppe*, landing at Sülte near Schwerin. *Gruppenkommandeur* Hauptmann Andreas Kuffner and Oberleutnant Rainer Nossek, *Staffelkapitän* of 3.(Pz)/SG 9, were both killed. Oberleutnant Wilhelm Bromen managed to bring down one of the attackers before he was himself shot down and seriously wounded. Bromen's victim, his sixth kill on the Fw 190, was one of the last to fall to the guns of a *Schlacht* pilot, for eight days later the war was over.

Some weeks prior to the final cessation of hostilities, however, the Eastern Front had at long last witnessed an influx of Fw 190 fighter reinforcements. Less than a month after Operation *Bodenplatte* (Baseplate), the ill-advised and costly New Year's day attack by the *Jagdwaffe* on Allied-occupied air bases in northwest Europe, elements of some ten *Jagdgeschwader*, including 11 Fw 190-equipped *Gruppen*, began transferring eastwards. There had, in fact, already been a couple of brief appearances by Fw 190s on *Luftflotte* 6's orders of battle on two previous occasions. III./JG 11 had accompanied the re-equipped IV./JG 54 into Poland at the end of June 1944. An even more intriguing entry a year earlier revealed one(!) Fw 190 night-fighter being operated by 8./NJG 200 alongside its handful of He 111s and Ju 88s in August 1943.

But it was not until mid-January

1945, with Russian armour already encroaching on German soil and Berlin soon to be directly threatened, that any meaningful transfer began. By then it was too late. With the Eastern and Western powers drawing ever closer together, and the Reich within weeks of being cut in two by American and Russian forces linking up on the River Elbe, it is arguable whether these latecomers can be classed as true 'Eastern Front' units. For although committed against the Soviets on paper, the majority had also to contend with the marauding Western Allies at their backs.

Ordered to East Prussia on 14 January, for example, I./JG 1 lost some dozen pilots killed or wounded to British fighters, arriving at Jürgenfelde only ten strong. Although claiming several Soviet aircraft destroyed, including a Yak-9 downed by *Gruppenkommandeur* Oberleutnant Emil Demuth on 30 January, they suffered five more casualties before their withdrawal in early February to retrain on the He 162 *Volksjäger*. II.Gruppe's introduction to Eastern Front conditions was little better. Losing two pilots killed in a clash with Yaks on the day of their arrival, they were then forced to blow up ten of their own aircraft in hasty retreats before the week was out.

Equipped with heavily armed and armoured Fw 190A-8/R8s, IV./JG 3 'Udet' was a Defence of the Reich *Sturmgruppe*, a dedicated anti-bomber unit. But it too was rushed eastwards and pressed into service bombing and strafing Soviet forces advancing along the Oder front towards Stettin and Berlin. Although even more impervious to ground fire than the normal A-8, the '*Sturmbock*' was no match for Russian fighters. But IV./JG 3's newly-appointed *Gruppenkommandeur*, Oberleutnant Oskar Romm – the same 'Ossi' Romm who had scored his first kills with I./JG 54 over Vyazma in December 1942 – was nothing if not resourceful.

He had first seen the penultimate model of the Focke-Wulf line, the long-nosed D-9 powered by a liquid-cooled Junkers Jumo engine, a few weeks earlier. And he now set about organising himself some of these new fighters; even to the extent of rescuing abandoned examples from bases about to be overrun by the enemy. He soon had enough to equip not just his *Stabsschwarm*, but an entire *Staffel* as well:

'As an air-superiority and interceptor fighter the Fw 190D-9 handled better than the Fw 190A. It was faster and had a superior rate of climb. In the dive it could leave the Russian Yak-3 and Yak-9 fighters standing.'

Romm's career on the 'Dora-9' was cut short on 24 April. Attacking a group of *Stormoviks* south of Stettin, he had sliced through their fighter escort without difficulty when his engine began to overheat. Diving steeply away, he outdistanced with ease the Russian fighters attempting to follow him, only

Otto Dommeratzky of 6./SG 2 is pictured here as an Oberfeldwebel in 1943. His Knight's Cross was awarded on 5 January 1943, and he was tragically killed on 13 October 1944. The Oak Leaves were awarded to Dommeratzky posthumously on 25 November 1944. He had scored close to 40 victories by the time of his death

The middle machine in this trio of Fw 190D-9s of IV./JG 3 seen at Prenzlau in March 1945 shows distinct signs of previous ownership – its rear fuselage band has been overpainted at some point in its recent past

'Ossi' Romm's personally scrounged 'Dora-9' (note *Gruppenkommandeur*'s double chevron just visible behind wing) outside a Prenzlau hangar in early 1945

to be seriously injured in a crash-landing back over his own lines.

Hauptmann Herbert Kutscha's III./JG 11 also returned to the east towards the end of January 1945, this time accompanied by the *Geschwaderstab* and I. *Gruppe* as well. Together they operated primarily along the Oder front and beyond, towards Posen (Poznan). But it was over Straussberg, near Berlin, on 17 February that they lost their *Geschwaderkommodore* when *Major* Jürgen Harder – formerly a Mediterranean Bf 109 ace – was killed in a crash caused, it is believed, by oxygen failure.

II./JG 300 was another A-8/R8 *'Sturmgruppe'* sent to the Eastern Front. Together with elements of JG 301 (a *Geschwader* which also possessed a number of D-9s, plus the only examples of the Ta 152H, the final development of the entire wartime Focke-Wulf fighter family, known to have entered operational service), it was ordered to the scene of the Russian breakthrough along the Oder on 1 February.

But the danger of having to wage war on two fronts was graphically demonstrated eight days later when the combined *Gruppen* were recalled to combat US bombers over western Germany and lost 11 of their number in the process. By April III./JG 301 were attacking American ground forces along the River Elbe, only to be ordered to about-turn once again. They ended their war in the defence of Berlin where, many witnesses report, they encountered captured, Russian-flown *'Dora-9s'* –'Ossi' Romm apparently didn't get them all!

While the majority of these 'new' Fw 190 *Gruppen* fought over the northern and eastern approaches of Berlin, others were being despatched to the southern sectors. JG 6's destination was lower Silesia. At Görlitz, as part of the *Gefechtsverband* Rudel, their II. *Gruppe* took on the unenviable task formerly performed by II./SG 2 – protecting the handful of obsolete anti-tank Ju 87s of SG 2 that were somehow still flying on a daily basis. *Stab* and I./JG 6 shared their Reichenberg base with a small tactical reconnaissance unit.

Romm's reserve aircraft wore the single chevron of the *Gruppen-Adjutant* – the latter was not qualified as a fighter pilot, and so never flew it himself whilst with IV./JG 3

Until the end of March JG 6's *Geschwaderkommodore* was Major Gerhard Barkhorn, the Luftwaffe's second-highest scorer. All 301 of Barkhorn's victories were achieved on the Eastern Front (with JG 52). It is perhaps indicative of the difficulties of those final days that the last of them had gone down on 5 January, 11 days before he assumed command of JG 6, and that he did not add a single one during the ten weeks he led the unit.

'FINIS'

While the newcomers from the west were learning the harsh realities of Eastern Front air warfare, the campaign veterans, JGs 51 and 54, were now both cut off with their backs to the Baltic Sea. By mid-March German forces in East Prussia had been pushed back into two pockets either side of Danzig Bay, one around the state capital Königsberg and the other around Danzig itself. They also held the 'Frische Nehrung', the long spit of land between the two. In mid-March JG 51's *Stabsstaffel* were based at Neutief out along this narrow spit. From here on 25 March they had downed seven Soviet bombers. Three days later the field came under heavy Russian artillary fire, directed from a tethered balloon on the mainland. Volunteers among the groundcrews struggled to keep the remaining Fw 190s serviced between the incoming salvoes. On 7 April the *Kapitän*, Leutnant Wilhelm Hübner, was killed by a direct flak hit over Neukuhren; he had scored 62 victories while with the *Staffel*. As Neutief was becoming completely untenable, the *Staffel* moved east into the shrinking Königsberg pocket. But their new base, Littausdorf, was soon under constant air attack from *Stormoviks*, Pe-2s and ground-strafing Airacobras. At the height of one such raid, on 15 April, a solitary Fw 190 managed to sneak in, miraculously surviving the exploding bombs and cannon fire. It was piloted by Major Heinz Lange, who had just flown alone over 250 miles of enemy held territory to take over from Major Fritz Losigkeit as the sixth and final *Kommodore* of JG 51. But Lange's sad duty was to do little more than oversee the dissolution of the *Geschwader*. On 28 April the *Stabsstaffel* was disbanded. Several pilots flew their aircraft out to the west; one enterprising young Unteroffizier even managed to take his girlfriend with him!

The disappearance of the *Geschwaderstab* allowed Lange to return whence he came: to the command of IV./JG 51. This *Gruppe* had just re-equipped with brand-new Fw 190A-8s, and even a few D-9s, at Garz, further west along the coast. Compared to the painstaking transition from Bf 109 to Fw 190 back in the winter of 1942-43, their recent 'conversion' could best be termed rudimentary. A civilian employee from the Focke-Wulf factory explained the cockpit layout to them, described the 190's handling characteristics, warned them *never* to lift the tail on take-off ... and that was it! After a few practice flights they were transferred south to the Berlin area. It says something about the men, or the machines – or both – that in three weeks they claimed 115 kills for the loss of 5 of their own.

On 29 April Major Heinz Lange was involved in his last dogfight,

Major Erich Rudorffer, *Gruppenkommandeur* of II./JG 54 for almost two years, is pictured here in August 1943, prior to being awarded the Oak Leaves and Swords. He survived the war to finish with an incredible 222 kills, 136 of which he claimed in the the east with JG 54

Father Christmas (aka Feldwebel Fritz Hangebrauk, Gerd Thyben's wing man) is welcomed by 7./JG 54 'black men' at Libau, in Courland, on Christmas Day 1944

Hauptmann Herbert Findeisen, replaced Rudorffer as *Gruppenkommandeur* of II./JG 54 in Courland 1945

Two newly decorated Knight's Cross wearers – (left) Leutnant Hermann Schleinhege (awarded on 19 February 1945), and (right) Leutnant Hugo Broch (awarded 12 March 1945). Both were from II./JG 54 at Schrunden (Cirava)/Courland, in March 1945

Seen at Libau-Nord, Leutnant Schulz gets the newly established 6.*Staffel*'s 100th kill in March 1945

with four La-7s over Neubrandenburg; but it fell to Oberfeldwebel Alfred Rauch to claim JG 51's final Fw 190 victory of the war on that same date. And on 1 May they suffered their last Fw 190 casualty when Oberfeldwebel Heinz Marquardt had to take to his parachute after an encounter with Spitfires north of the German capital. The following day they retired to Flensburg and British captivity. For the Fw 190s of JG 51 the war was over.

Which left just *Jagdgeschwader* 54.

And they had their own private war raging on their doorstep. But despite – or perhaps because of – their sense of isolation, I. and II./JG 54's scores continued to mount during their final months trapped up on the Courland peninsula. On 15 October 1944, the eve of the first Russian attempt to overrun the pocket, Oberleutnant Helmut Wettstein, *Staffelkapitän* of 6./JG 54, had achieved the *Geschwader*'s 8000th victory. In all the Soviets would hurl six separate offensives against the defenders of Courland. By the close of the second, on 28 November, JG 54 had claimed another 239 kills. On just two days during the course of the third, which lasted from 21 to 31 December, they achieved 100 victories at the cost of 11 to themselves. But every casualty was deeply felt. A sad blow on the opening day of third Courland was the loss of 3.*Staffel*'s Leutnant Hans-Joachim Kroschinski. A member of I./JG 54 since the summer of 1942, 'Kroschi' was on the point of downing the last of five Pe-2s – bringing his total to 76 – when its rear gunner bracketed his Fw 190. The forward fuel tank immediately burst into flames and an explosive shell shattered Kroschinski's ankle.

Despite his wound, and the flames searing into the cockpit, he somehow managed to bale out. He was unconscious when he hit the ground. He survived, but only at the cost of his sight and the loss of a leg. Six days later an even longer serving pilot was lost when Leutnant Heinz 'Piepl' Wernicke, a 112-victory *Experte* leading 1.*Staffel*, was accidentally rammed by his *Katschmarek* during a dogfight southwest of Riga.

The comparative lull in the ground fighting between each Soviet offensive offered some semblance of a respite for the weary Courland army. But for JG 54's two *Gruppen* there were no such let-ups. The Russian air force attacked the peninsula's supply and evacuation ports without pause. The

main harbour in particular, Libau, suffered raid after heavy raid. II./JG 54 based at nearby Libau-Grobin, and I. *Gruppe* some 40 miles inland at Schrunden, took a steady toll of the attackers. On two consecutive days during one such 'lull' in mid-December, they claimed 44 and 56 enemy aircraft destroyed during massed raids on Libau's town and dock areas. When not defending the supply ports, they were protecting the ships themselves as they ran the

The *6.Staffel Schwarm* which sank two Soviet MTBs off Bad Polangen, in the Courland Peninsula, in March 1945. Left to right, Feldwebel Meschkat, Unteroffizier Licht, Leutnant Hannig and Unteroffizier Kohler

gauntlet of Soviet air and sea attack. They also provided fighter escort for Courland's few '*Mausis*' – lumbering Ju 52s, each with a large dural hoop beneath fuselage and wings – as they swept the sea approaches to the peninsula for enemy mines.

The pressure never eased. On 24 January 1945 the Russians launched their fourth offensive; on 20 February their fifth. It was during February that JG 54 lost two leading personalities. The first came about with the transfer of Major Erich Rudorffer to the command of II./JG 7. Rudorffer had been *Gruppenkommandeur* of II./JG 54 ever since the death of Hauptmann Jung over Mga back in July 1943. Previously a member of JG 2 in the west and the Mediterranean, he quickly began adding to his already considerable number of victories after arrival in Russia.

An expert marksman, the quiet, retiring Rudorffer may be ranked alongside the likes of the more extrovert Nowotny, Hartmann and Marseille. But he outshone them all in terms of multiple daily kills. His most outstanding feat of gunnery occurred on 6 November 1943 when he shot down 13 Soviet aircraft in the course of one 17-minute engagement! Rudorffer survived the war with his final score standing at 222. But this figure had not been achieved without incident. He was himself shot down on 16 occasions and had to bale out nine times; the latter feat alone more than enough to earn him his paratrooper's wings! For the final three months of the war Rudorffer's place at the head of II./JG 54 was taken by Hauptmann Herbert 'Mungo' Findeisen, who added 25 kills during that

Feldwebel Meschkat climbs out of his Fw 190A-8 after the above-mentioned MTB mission

A Soviet G-class MTB comes under air attack in the Baltic

time to the 47 he had earlier scored over Russia as a reconnaissance pilot.

The *Geschwader*'s second major loss of February 1945 hit the 'Green Hearts' hard. It was the death of the highest scoring of them all. Another quiet and serious type, the slow-spoken Otto Kittel had joined 2./JG 54 as an NCO pilot in the autumn of 1941. His early days on the Bf 109 gave no indication of the success that was to come. It took him some eight months to achieve his first 15 kills, and another nine to

The commanders meet – left to right, Oberst Dieter Hrabak (*Geschwaderkommodore* JG 54), Hauptmann Helmut Wettstein (*Staffelkapitän* 6./JG 54), Major Herbert Findeisen (*Gruppenkommandeur* II./JG 54) and Generaloberst Kurt Pflugbeil, AOC *Luftflotte* 1, are seen at Libau-Nord in February 1945

Although not an escapee from Courland, the NCO just visible in the aft fuselage radio compartment nevertheless gives some idea of the cramped conditions experienced by the occupant, even without the hatch screwed back on!

add two dozen more. But number 59 in February 1943 marked not just the 4000th for the *Geschwader*, it also heralded Feldwebel Otto Kittel's rise to fame. Recently converted to the Fw 190, thereafter he never looked back. In just over a year his score stood at 150. And despite being shot down twice – and suffering two weeks of Soviet captivity, from which he managed to escape – it had continued to rise ever since.

On 14 February Oberleutnant Otto Kittel scrambled to intercept a formation of incoming *Stormoviks*. But on this, his 583rd combat mission, luck finally deserted him. He was killed by return fire from one of the Ilyushins' rear-gunners. With a total score of 267 confirmed victories, Otto Kittel was the Luftwaffe's fourth highest ranking ace. Over Courland his name was known in the forwardmost trenches. As a member of his *Staffel* said, 'When Otto Kittel was killed, for us darkness fell in the Courland pocket.'

And he was right. The following month, on 18 March, the sixth and final Soviet onslaught began. Once more it was blunted and stopped. But when Adolf Hitler – the one man at whose insistence the Courland peninsula had been held for all these months – committed suicide in Berlin on 30 April, there died with him all thoughts of using the 'fortress' of Courland as the jumping-off point for a last-minute counter-attack.

The capitulation of Germany, and the surrender of all her armed forces, was only days away. For the Luftwaffe units in Courland this meant one thing: escape to the west, taking as many of their comrades with them as they could. The '*Mausis*' repaid JG 54's previous services by loading their departing Ju 52s with fighter groundcrew in addition to their own. The C-in-C of *Luftflotte* 1, Generaloberst Kurt Pflugbeil – 'Papi' Pflugbeil to his men – placed his own Ju 52 at their disposal, preferring to see it used to evacuate more ground personnel while he, together with his staff, elected to stay behind and endure many years of Soviet captivity.

The Fw 190 pilots also helped their own. Some 50 aircraft left Courland, stripped of equipment but packed with two, three or even four occupants. The faces of those who watched one Fw 190 land safely

The end in the north saw dozens of Fw 190As and Ds (plus a solitary Bf 109), mostly minus propellers, parked at Flensburg, and photographed from the elevated vantage point of a dumped Ju 52 'Mausi'

An upturned 'Mausi' of 2./Minensuchgruppe der Luftwaffe (3K+CK) rests on 'Yellow C', a Schlacht Fw 190 almost certainly of III./SG 3, a Gruppe which shared the last days in Courland with JG 54

in the west and saw *five* people emerge – two squashed behind the pilot, one from the rear fuselage radio compartment and one from each wing ammunition bay – were, by all accounts, something to behold!

A few 'Green Hearts' made for their home towns. One or two opted for neutral Sweden less than 200 miles away across the Baltic. But the majority followed orders directing them to fly to British-held Flensburg or Kiel in Schleswig-Holstein. Among the latter, one of the last to leave was the *Staffelkapitän* of 7./JG 54, Oberleutnant Gerhard Thyben. Prior to joining the *Geschwader* a little over a year earlier, Thyben had served with JG 3. He had scored his 100th victory on 30 September 1944, and had since added another 56.

Early on the morning of 8 May Thyben took off, his chief mechanic Albert Mayers crammed into the radio compartment behind him trying hard not to disturb the tail control rods and cables running the length of the fuselage. With his *Katschmarek,* Feldwebel Fritz Hangebrauk, tucked alongside, the two Fw 190s set course westwards. As they headed out over open water, the smoke and ruins of Libau began to slip away behind them. Suddenly, ahead and below, Gerd Thyben spotted a dark green Petlyakov . . .

The end on the central front – Fw 190 carcasses litter the apron of Berlin's huge Tempelhof airport, which was used throughout the war as a storage and repair facility for all manner of Luftwaffe aircraft

1

Fw 190A-8 'Black Double Chevron' of Hauptmann Paul-Heinrich Dähne, *Gruppenkommandeur* II./JG 1, Mecklenburg, circa February 1945

Representative of the influx of Fw 190s to the Eastern Front in 1945, Dähne's machine displays one of the typical styles of late-war camouflage and national insignia. The retention of JG 1's Defence of the Reich red aft fuselage band indicates that it was probably among the earliest batch of transferees in mid-January and Dähne may well have inherited it from the previous *Gruppenkommandeur* at the time of the move, Major Hermann Staiger. Dähne himself scored 100+ victories, some 80 of them in the east (he had served with JG 52 in 1942/43) but, in the absence of log books or unit diaries, it is impossible to establish exactly how many were gained on Fw 190s in 1945. He was killed on 24 April 1945 flying the Heinkel He 162 *Volksjäger*.

2

Fw 190A-8 'Yellow 1' of Major Bernd Gallowitsch, *Staffelkapitän* 7./JG 1, Garz/Usedom, March 1945

Unlike Dähne's aircraft, Gallowitsch's 'Anton-8' wears no Defence of the Reich band. Probably a replacement delivered after the *Gruppe*'s arrival in the east, note too the completely different, closely dappled camouflage finish and national insignia presentation. After a varied career, including servcie with JG 51 in Russia, Gallowitch ended the war with 64 kills, all but 5 of which he claimed in the east. Again, it is unknown just how many he scored on the Fw 190 during the closing months.

3

Fw 190D-9 'Black Double Chevron' of Oberleutnant Oskar Romm, *Gruppenkommandeur* IV./JG 3, Prenzlau, March 1945

Romm's aircraft displays standard, almost pristine camouflage and markings of the period, including a carefully outlined *Kommandeur*'s double chevron. This was in contrast with many of *Stab* IV./JG 3's 'Dora-9's which showed heavy wear and evidence of much repainting to cover traces of previous ownership. None, however, appears to have been given any form of IV.*Gruppe* identity marking aft of the fuselage cross. Romm's wartime career also ended in a crash on 24 April 1945 (see Dähne above) in which he was severely injured; his score at the time standing at 92.

4

Fw 190D-9 'Black Chevron and Bars' of Oberstleutnant Gerhard Michalski, *Geschwaderkommodore* JG 4, Oder Front, circa January 1945

Wearing a slightly unusual dapple scheme, this was one of several similarly marked 'D-9s' flown by Michalski during the winter of 1944/45. The *Kommodore*'s insignia, consisting of a single chevron with a bar each side of the fuselage cross, dates back to pre-war biplane days. Note the overpainting of JG 54's black-white-black Defence

of the Reich bands, evidence of recent transfer from the Rhine to the Oder Front. A long-time member of II./JG 53, and a Bf 109 Mediterranean ace, Michalski ended the war with 14 Eastern Front kills, only to lose his life in a road accident nine months later.

5

Fw 190A-3 'Black 1' of Hauptmann Friedrich-Wilhelm Strakeljahn, *Staffelkapitän* 14. (Jabo)/JG 5, Petsamo/northern Finland, circa June 1943

Early standard finish Fw 190 with no (or prior to application of) yellow Eastern Front theatre markings, but note the 'bow and bomb' *Staffel* badge on the cowling; very much the exception rather than the rule on eastern-based Fw 190s after the spring of 1943. Strakeljahn took his *Staffel* to Italy in the spring of 1944, but returned to the Russian Front that same summer as *Gruppenkommandeur* of II./SG 4. He was killed in action on 6 July 1944. Although primarily a fighter-bomber exponent throughout, he nevertheless managed also to score at least 9 aerial victories.

6

Fw 190D-9 'Black Chevron and Bars of Major Gerhard Barkhorn, *Geschwaderkommodore* JG 6, Lower Silesia, circa January 1945

Wearing similar insignia to Michalski's, Barkhorn's 'Dora-9' is included by default, for although he was the Luftwaffe's second-ranking ace with 301 Eastern Front kills to his credit, he didn't score a single one on the Fw 190. His aircraft does, however, show JG 6's finish and markings of the period including, it is claimed, the red-white-red bands indicating the unit's Defence of the Reich duties immediately prior to its transfer eastwards. It also displays his wife's name, *Christl*, below the cockpit sill and a tiny 'white 5' in the angle of the chevron, both dating back to the Bf 109F he flew at the start of the campaign.

7

Fw 190A-8 'Black Double Chevron' of Hauptmann Herbert Kutscha, *Gruppenkommandeur* III./JG 11, Brandenburg, circa February 1945

Another late war finish incorporating simplified national insignia is illustrated by Kutscha's A-8. It also features the unit's previous Defence of the Reich aft fuselage band. Being yellow – the colour of the official Eastern Front theatre markings – little attempt was made to obliterate these bands on being transferred eastwards during the latter part of January 1945. Having scored his first kill as early as 14 December 1939 (a Wellington over the German Bight), Kutscha subsequently saw service as a *Zerstörer* and close-support pilot. He ended the war with 47 victories, 14 of them against the Soviets, plus many ground targets destroyed.

8

Fw 190A-3 'Black Double Chevron' of Hauptmann Heinrich Krafft *Gruppenkommandeur* I./JG 51,

Jesau/East Prussia, August 1942
The A-3s assigned to I./JG 51 during their conversion on to the type at Jesau wore standard camouflage and markings of the period but, as yet, no Eastern Front yellow theatre bands. Many did, however, display the *Gruppe* badge as shown here, a stylised chamois on a mountain peak. This badge did not long survive the transfer to Russia, where such indentifiable enblems would soon be forbidden. 'Gaudi' Krafft did not himself survive long either, being downed by flak on 14 December with his score standing at 78.

9

Fw 190-A-5 'Black Double Chevron' of Major Erich Leie, *Gruppenkommandeur* I./JG 51, Orel, Circa May 1943
I.*Gruppe's* third Fw 190 *Kommandeur*, Erich Leie, was more fortunate than his predecessors, remaining at the helm for almost two years. His A-5, pictured here prior to the Kursk offensive, has abandoned winter white for the two-tone splinter green of early summer. Note too that the yellow theatre marking, previously centred behind the fuselage cross, has now moved to the aft position immediately forward of the tail unit. Promoted *Geschwaderkommodore* of JG 77 at the end of 1944, Leie was killed over Czechoslovakia on 7 March 1945 when he collided with a crashing Yak-9 and failed to survive a low-level bale out. He had scored 75 Eastern Front kills, plus 43 in the west.

10

Fw 190A-3 'Black Double Chevron' of Hauptmann Rudolf Busch, *Gruppenkommandeur* I./JG 51, Lake Ivan/Russia, January 1943
The 'Anton-3' of Krafft's successor, Hauptmann Rudolf Busch, demonstrates what just a few weeks hard campaigning can do. The recently applied white winter finish is already stained and weathered from operations and dispersal in the open on the frozen surface of Lake Ivan. Yellow theatre markings have been added, but note that the *Gruppe* badge has now disappeared. After little more than a month in command of I.*Gruppe*, Busch was killed in a collision during take-off from Lake Ivan on 17 January 1943. He had achieved some 40 victories, all but 5 of them in the east.

11

Fw 190A-3 'Yellow 9' of Hauptmann Heinz Lange, *Staffelkapitän* 3./JG 51, Vyazma, December 1942
Back to the depths of winter for Lange's A-3, which has been given a temporary coat of patchy winter white overall. From *Kapitän* of 3./JG 51 Heinz Lange rose, *via Kommandeur* of IV.*Gruppe*, to become JG 51's sixth and final *Kommodore* less than four weeks before the end of the war. He had begun his career with I./JG 51, shooting down an RAF Blenheim near the German-Dutch border on 30 October 1939. To this single western kill he subsequently added 69 more during nearly four years' service on the Eastern Front.

12

Fw 190A-4 'Yellow 1 of Oberfeldwebel Herbert Bareuther, 3./JG 51, Orel, June 1943

Another I.*Gruppe* machine pictured about the time of *Zitadelle*, Bareuther's 'Yellow 1' shows marked differences in finish from Leie's A-5 above. Note that 3.*Staffel's* individual aircraft numerals were of a very dark yellow shade, often described as 'brown'. Bareuther subsequently joined Oskar Romm's IV./JG 3, and was killed on 30 April 1945 leading that unit's 14.*Staffel* in a low-level attack on Soviet forces north of Prenzlau. His final score stood at 55, all gained in the east.

13

Fw 190A-4 'Yellow 5' of Leutnant Josef Jennewein, 3./JG 51, Orel, June 1943
Dsplaying yet another variety of finish, Jennewein's A-4 wears a segment camouflage scheme variously described as brown, or tan, and green. Again note the deep yellow of the numeral in comparison to the aft fuselage band. '5' was Jennewein's lucky number. It was the numeral he was wearing when he won the 1940 combined slalom, downhill and alpine World Ski Championship.

14

Fw 190A-5 'Black Double Chevron' of Hauptmann Fritz Losigkeit, *Gruppenkommandeur* III./JG 51, Kursk, July 1943
One of the earliest machines flown by Losigkeit during his ten months at the head of III./JG 51, this slightly lighter than usual A-5 wears standard markings and insignia of the period, including the vertical III.*Gruppe* bar immediately forward of the aft fuselage yellow theatre band. Promoted to *Kommodore* in April 1944, he remained in that post for a further year before assuming command of JG 77 in the final weeks of the war. All but about a dozen of his 68 victories were achieved during his service in the east with JG 51.

15

Fw 190A-3 'White 11' of Hauptmann Herbert Wehnelt, *Staffelkapitän* 7./JG 51, Orel, circa January 1943
Its coat of winter white already showing distinct signs of wear and tear, Wehnelt's 'White 11' has also had the upper part of its aft fuselage yellow theatre band painted over to reduce visibility from above; a pointer that air attacks on JG 51's bases were beginning to make themselves felt. Wehnelt scored all 36 of his kills with JG 51 (including 2 in the west) before being promoted to the command of *Ergänzungsgruppe* West in August 1943.

16

Fw 190D-9 'White 1' of Leutnant Kurt Tanzer, *Staffelkapitän* 13./JG 51, Schmoldow/Pomerania, April 1945
After a long period on Bf 109s, IV./JG 51 reverted to Focke-Wulfs in the closing weeks of the war. Both A-8s and D-9s wore the standard finishes of the period, and all carried the wavy bar *Gruppe* marking aft of the cross as depicted here, but they no longer displayed any yellow theatre colouring. Tanzer himself scored 126 of his 143 victories in the east. He rejoined the post-war *Bundesluftwaffe*, only to be killed in a T-33 trainer in 1960.

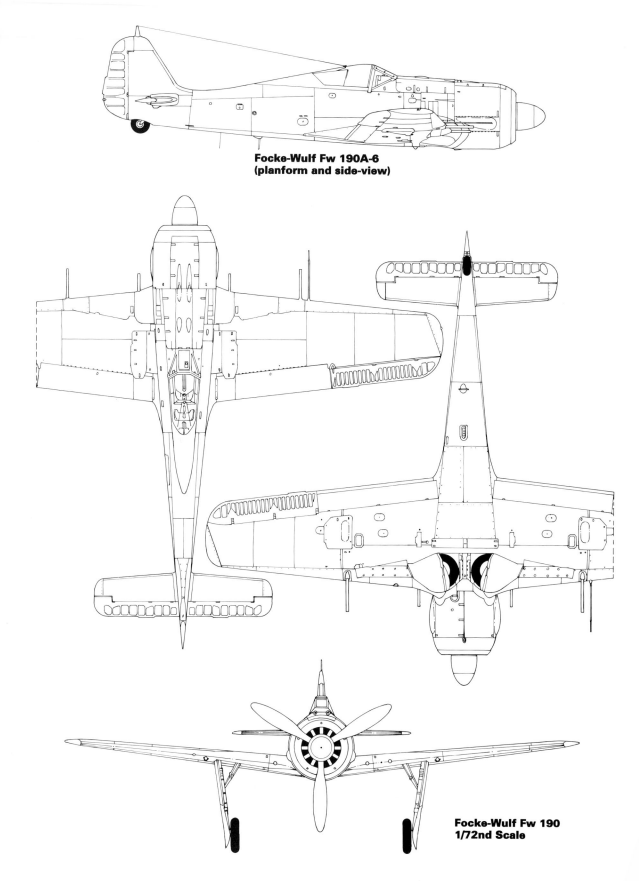

Focke-Wulf Fw 190A-6
(planform and side-view)

Focke-Wulf Fw 190
1/72nd Scale

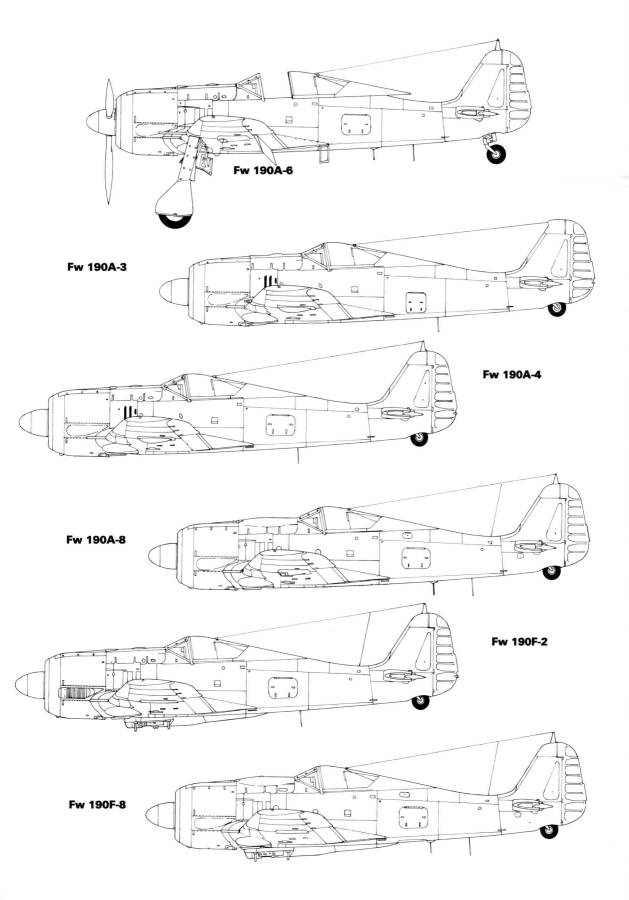

Fw 190A-6

Fw 190A-3

Fw 190A-4

Fw 190A-8

Fw 190F-2

Fw 190F-8

17

Fw 190A-8 'Black 3 and Bars' of Unteroffizier Helmut Johne, *Stabsstaffel* JG 51, Memel, November 1944

While the three Eastern Front *Gruppen* of JG 51 converted from their early Focke-Wulfs back to the Bf 109 in 1943-4, the *Stabsstaffel* remained on Fw 190s during the whole of their time in the east. Their *Staffel* markings also remained constant throughout, consisting, in effect, of a *Geschwaderkommodore's* insignia of a bar either side of the fuselage cross (the forward one pointed), but with the latter's chevron replaced by a black individual number. The significance of the yellow spinner and nose ring is unknown, unless perhaps they served as a recognition aid for German flak and ground troops who were becoming notoriously quick on the trigger by this stage of the war, so unused were they to seeing 'friendlies' overhead: 'If it's uncamouflaged it's American, if it's camouflaged it's Russian, if it's invisible it's German!' Johne's score stood at eight Soviet aircraft destroyed before he was himself shot down (by the enemy!) on 9 February 1945.

18

Fw 190A-8 'Black 6 and Bars' of Oberfeldwebel Fritz Lüddecke, *Stabsstaffel* JG 51, Orscha, circa July 1944

For a brief period earlier in 1944 the *Stabsstaffel* had also taken to decorating their A-8s with personal names (presumably of wives or girlfriends), a highly unusual practice for Eastern Front 190s. Note that unlike the other three *Stabsstaffel* machines illustrated, 'Hanni' does not have her markings outlined in white. A 50-victory *'Experte'* also renowned for numerous close-support and fighter bomber missions, 'Paule' Lüddecke succumbed to flak over the Lithuanian/-East Prussian border on 10 August 1944.

19

Fw 190A-8 'Black 11 and Bars' of Leutnant Günther Heym, *Stabsstaffel* JG 51, Zichenau, circa September 1944

Günther Heym's *Tanja* (*Tania*) has a distinctly oriental flavour about her. She certainly brought him luck as of the four *Stabsstaffel* pilots depicted here, Heym – with over 20 kills to his credit – was the only one to survive the final stages of the war.

20

Fw 190A-8 'Black 12 and Bars' of *Feldwebel* Johann Merbeler, *Stabsstaffel* JG 51, Neukuhren/East Prussia, November 1944

Last of the quartet, Merbeler's A-8 had reverted to nameless anonymity by the late autumn of 1944. Having downed a dozen enemy aircraft as a member of the *Stabsstaffel*, Merbeler was reported missing early in January 1945.

21

Fw 190A-4 'Black Double Chevron and Bars' of Oberstleutnant Hannes Trautloft, *Geschwaderkommodore* JG 54, Krasnogvardeisk, circa December 1942

Already showing signs of weathering, the white winter camouflage of the *Kommodore's* A-4 is further compromised by the colourful yellow theatre markings and elaborate emblem. This latter consists of the 'Green Heart', introduced by Trautloft himself, with the coats-of-arms of the home bases of JG 54's three component *Gruppen* superimposed: top left, Nuremberg (I.); top right, Vienna-Aspern (II.) and bottom – with three Bf 109 silhouettes added – Jesau (III.). These badges would soon disappear, an official edict early in 1943 prohibiting all such identifying markings on Eastern Front aircraft. Although seemingly ignored by a number of Bf 109 units, this order – together with another discouraging personal scores from being displayed - was apparently strictly adhered to by JG 54. It is not known why Trautloft opted for the command insignia shown here, an unusual combination of a *Gruppenkommandeur's* double chevron with a *Kommodore's* horizontal bars. At the head of JG 54 for almost three years, Trautloft scored 45 Eastern Front victories before promotion to a General Staff position.

22

Fw 190A-4 'White Chevron and Bars' of Major Hubertus von Bonin, *Geschwaderkommodore* JG 54, Krasnogvardeisk, circa August 1943

In contrast to the above 'Anton-4', von Bonin's machine bears standard early style *Kommodore's* insignia, but note the small 'white 7' above the aft bar. It wears a solid dapple camouflage and full Eastern Front theatre markings, but is now minus the 'Green Heart'. Henceforth, the only clue to unit identity would be provided by JG 54's unique positioning of the yellow fuselage band directly behind the fuselage cross – JG 51 appear to have dropped their earlier practice of doing likewise in favour of the more usual aft fuselage position.

23

Fw 190A-5 'White Chevron and Bars' of Major Hubertus von Bonin, *Geschwaderkommodore* JG 54, Central Sector, circa November 1943

A later machine of von Bonin's displays a similar camouflage scheme with minor variations in the markings. Note that the small 'white 7' above the aft bar has now given way to a 'black 4'. Their significance is not known. It seems unlikely that they are 'lucky' talismans, and the sequence would seem to rule out their referring to the number of machines von Bonin got through during his tenure of office! One explanation could be that during this period all *Stabsschwarm* aircraft carried *Kommodore* insignia (plus a small numeral to differentiate between them) in order to confuse the enemy in the air, and that von Bonin simply used whichever happened to be serviceable. Von Bonin was the only *Kommodore* JG 54 lost to enemy action. He was killed near Vitebsk on 15 December 1943 after achieving 64 Eastern Front victories.

24

Fw 190A-6 'White Chevron and Bars of Oberstleutnant Anton Mader, *Geschwaderkommodore* JG 54, Dorpat/Estonia, July 1944

Von Bonin's successor, Anton Mader, has retained the white command chevron and bars. But his machine wears a completely different camouflage scheme of faded brown and green, a combination particularly suited to the northern sector and also to be found on many of *Luftflotte* 1's reconnaissance aircraft. Altogether Mader claimed a total of 86 kills, about 25 of them during prior service in the western and Mediterranean theatres.

25
Fw 190A-4 'Black Double Chevron' of Hauptmann Hans Philipp, *Gruppenkommandeur* I./JG 54, Krasnogvardeisk, circa January 1943
Freshly painted in winter white, Philipp's A-4 wears full fig theatre markings, command insignia and unit badges. I.*Gruppe*'s machines did not remain this pristine for long. Having scored his first kill over Poland in 1939 with JG 76, 'Fips' Philipp went on to become the second pilot to reach the 200-victory mark (on 17 March 1943). He left JG 54 a fortnight later to assume command of JG 1 in the west and was shot down by US P-47s on 8 October 1943 when his total was standing at 206, all but 29 scored on the Russian Front.

26
Fw 190A-6 'Black Double Chevron' of Hauptmann Walter Nowotny, *Gruppenkommandeur* I./JG 54, Vitebsk, November 1943
The machine in which Nowotny scored his 250th victory (on 14 October 1943) making him the Luftwaffe's leading ace of the time, Werk-Nr. 410004 has had its standard grey camouflage finish heavily overpainted in two shades of green. Note the small 'white 8' in the angle of the command chevrons (believed to be a reference to an earlier favourite aircraft) and Nowotny's additional 'lucky 13' below the cockpit sill. Walter Nowotny relinquished command of I./JG 54 in February 1944, first to take over a training unit and then to head the experimental Me 262 jet fighter unit which bore his name. He died in a crash at Achmer on 8 November 1944 after an engagement with US heavy bombers and their fighter escort. 255 of his 258 confirmed victories were scored in the east; a further 22 remain unconfirmed.

27
Fw 190A-8 'Black Double Chevron' of Hauptmann Franz Eisenach, *Gruppenkommandeur* I./JG 54, Schrunden/Courland, circa November 1944
I.*Gruppe*'s last *Kommandeur* of the war, Eisenach flew this remarkably well-preserved (or newly delivered?) 'Anton-8' during the height of the Courland battles. It wears a standard finish of the time and features a simplified fuselage cross and spiral spinner. Originally a *Zerstörer* pilot, all 129 of Eisenach's kills were achieved in the east.

28
Fw 190A-4 'White 8' of Leutnant Walter Nowotny, *Staffelkapitän* 1./JG 54, Krasnogvardeisk, November 1942
Another well-documented machine, in stark contrast to the majority of the anonymous and unidentifiable 190s flown on the Eastern Front by all and sundry – or at least by whoever's name happened to be next on the ops board) – this is the aircraft in which Nowotny scored his *Staffel*'s 300th victory of the war. The toned-down (or simply dirty?) white of the fuselage cross seems an unnecessary precaution on an otherwise standard white winter camouflaged A-4.

29
Fw 190A-4 'White 10' of Leutnant Walter Nowotny, *Staffelkapitän* 1./JG 54, Krasnogvardeisk, Spring 1943
The spring thaw of 1943 is reflected in the finish of this A-4, also flown on occasion by Nowotny. The white winter camouflage has been partially removed leaving a green-white segment finish ideally suited to blend in with the terrain below. Note I.*Gruppe*'s badge and the 'Green Heart' are still being worn, but not for much longer.

30
Fw 190A-5 'White 5' of Oberleutnant Walter Nowotny, *Staffelkapitän* 1./JG 54, Krasnogvardeisk, circa June 1943
By June, the month in which Nowotny scored his 100th over Nowa-Ladoga, both *Gruppe* badge and *Geschwader* emblem were gone. This heavily mottled A-5 flown by Nowotny graphically illustrates the anonymity which cloaked JG 54's machines from mid-1943 onwards

31
Fw 190A-6 'White 12' of Leutnant Helmut Wettstein, *Staffelkapitän* 1./JG 54, Central Sector, 1943
Devoid of all unit markings, the A-6 flown by Nowotny's successor at the head of 1.*Staffel* wears the two-tone green splinter camouflage finish which typified I./JG 54's aircraft in the high summer of 1943. Wettstein subsequently transferred back to II.*Gruppe*, where he served as *Staffelkapitän* of 6./JG 54 until the war's end.

32
Fw 190A-8 'White 1' of Leutnant Heinz Wernicke, *Staffelkapitän* 1./JG 54, Riga-Skulte/Latvia, circa September 1944
Wearing a typical late wartime finish with simplified fuselage cross and tail swastika, Wernicke's 'Anton-8' is distinguished only by its surprisingly clean individual number, the latter apparently having been applied over a previous two-digit identity. Having started his career with I./JG 54 in the spring of 1942, all 117 of 'Piepl' Wernicke's victories were achieved while with this unit. He was killed in a mid-air collision with his wingman over Courland on 27 December 1944.

33
Fw 190A-8 'White 12' of Oberleutnant Josef Heinzeller, *Staffelkapitän* 1./JG 54, Schrunden/-Courland, November 1944
Another drab, late war A-8, this Fw 190 wears a different style of cross to the above, but it too displays 1.*Staffel*'s white spinner spiral of the period. Heinzeller ended the war with 35 kills.

34
Fw 190A-4 'White 9' of Feldwebel Karl Schnörrer, 1./JG 54, Krasnogvardeisk, circa January 1943

Nowotny's long-time wing man, 'Quax' Schnörrer often flew the winter camouflaged 'White 9' during the early months of 1943. Here it wears a near textbook set of national, theatre and unit markings; all that is lacking is the yellow segment sometimes applied to the lower rudder. Severely injured on 12 November 1943 with his Eastern Front score standing at 35, Schnörrer subsequently returned to operations on the Me 262 jet fighter. He added nine four-engined bombers to his total while with JG 7, but was again seriously wounded when shot down over Hamburg on 30 March 1945.

35

Fw 190A-4 'White 2' of Oberfeldwebel Anton Döbele, 1./JG 54, Krasnogvardeisk, Spring 1943
Another member of the famous 'Nowotny Schwarm', Anton Döbele flew this 'White 2' with the winter camouflage partially removed to suit the season of melting snow. Although the 'Green Heart' has been retained, the Gruppe badge on the engine cowling has already been overpainted. Döbele's death on 11 November 1943, when he was accidentally rammed by another German fighter near Vitebsk, signalled the end of the Schwarm's run of 524 victories (Schnörrer was wounded the following day). 'Toni' Döbele had himself scored a total of 94 Eastern Front kills.

36

Fw 190A-4 'White 3' of Feldwebel Peter Bremer, 1./JG 54, Orel, July 1943
Another example of I.Gruppe's two-tone green summer camouflage, Bremer's 'Anton-4' crash-landed behind enemy lines at the height of the Battle of Kursk on 13 July 1943. At the time of his capture Bremer had scored 40 kills in the east.

37

Fw 190A-4 'Black 5' of Hauptmann Hans Götz, Staffelkapitän 2./JG 54, circa July 1943
Götz's A-4 illustrates a variation on the summer camouflage theme with a slightly less well defined combination of the two greens. Note that the second Staffel of both JG 54's two Eastern Front Fw 190 Gruppen (i.e. 2./JG 54 and 5./JG 54) carried black and not red individual numerals as was previously the norm. The use of red had been banned (in a move similar to that taken by the Allied air forces in the Pacific theatre) to avoid any possible confusion with the markings worn by the enemy. Having joined 2./JG 54 back in January 1940, Götz's success did not begin until after his arrival in Russia, where he scored all of his 82 kills before being lost in action on 4 August 1943.

38

Fw 190A-4 'Black 11' of Feldwebel Hans-Joachim Kroschinski, 2./JG 54, Krasnogvardeisk, February 1943
Back to winter-camouflaged A-4s, this example showing distinct signs of use and weathering. A long-serving member of I.Gruppe, Kroschinski had claimed 75 Soviet aircraft destroyed – plus one US heavy bomber downed while serving as an instructor in the west – before being wounded over Courland on 24 December 1944.

39

Fw 190A-6 'Yellow 5' of Oberleutnant Otto Kittel, 3./JG 54, Riga-Skulte, circa August 1944
In keeping with Eastern Front anonymity, there is nothing to distinguish this perfectly standard A-6 as being the mount of JG 54's most successful pilot. The self-effacing Otto Kittel spent his entire 3½-year frontline career in the east with the 'Green Hearts'. Having achieved less than 40 kills during his early months on the Bf 109, the vast bulk of his final total of 267 confirmed victories were scored with the Focke-Wulf, making him arguably the greatest Fw 190 Ace of the Russian Front of them all! Kittel was killed over Courland on 14 February 1945 in action against that nemesis of so many Fw 190 pilots, the Stormovik.

40

Fw 190A-5 'Yellow 8' of Leutnant Robert Weiss, 3./JG 54, Orel, circa June 1943
Previously a member of JG 26 in the west, 'Bazi' Weiss then spent some two years in Russia before returning to the Reich to assume command of the 'Green Hearts' western-based Gruppe, III./JG 54, at whose head he was killed in action against Spitfires near the German-Dutch border on 29 December 1944. It is believed that some 90 out of his final total of 121 victories were scored on the Eastern Front, the majority on Fw 190s such as the two-tone green example depicted here.

41

Fw 190A-6 'Black Double Chevron' of Major Erich Rudorffer, Gruppenkommandeur II./JG 54, Immola/Finland, June 1944
Depicted at the time of his Gruppe's brief deployment to Finland, Rudorffer's closely dappled A-6 wears narrow-bordered Kommandeur chevrons, enclosing a small 'black 1', and matching II.Gruppe bar aft of the cross. Note the spiral spinner and light tail surfaces. The 'Green Heart's' overall third-ranking ace (after Kittel and Nowotny), 136 out of Rudorffer's tally of 222 kills were claimed on Fw 190s in the east. Belying his quiet nature, Rudorffer's was an incident-packed war which he ended with 12 kills on the Me 262.

42

Fw 190A-6 'Black 5' of Oberleutnant Max Stotz, 5./JG 54, Siverskaya, late Spring 1943
Recently freed of their winter white, many II.Gruppe aircraft were given a distinctive new camouflage scheme combining what has been described as tan, or brown, with two shades of green. Note that both Geschwader and Gruppe bagdes are still being worn, and also the black Staffel number. Stotz was promoted to Kapitän of 5./JG 54 later that same summer, only to be reported missing in action near Vitebsk on 19 August 1943. All but 16 of his 189 kills were gained with II.Gruppe.

43

Fw 190A-6 'Black 7' of Leutnant Emil Lang, 5./JG 54, Northern Sector, Summer 1943
Whether the paint II./JG 54 was using actually was official desert tan has not been established, but

Lang's machine graphically demonstrates that it too quickly faded. Compared with 'Black 5' above, it presents a much lighter overall appearance. Note also that all identifying badges have now been overpainted. 'Bully' Lang scored 173 kills, including 25 gained in the west after his promotion to command II./JG 26. He was killed in a dogfight with P-47s over Belgium on 3 September 1944.

44
Fw 190A-4 'Black 12' of Fähnrich Norbert Hannig, 5/JG 54, Siverskaya, circa May 1943
Another example of II.Gruppe's summer uniform of light brown and greens is illustrated by 5. Staffel's 'Black 12'. Presumably a more recent replacement machine, it never wore the unit badges of the earlier months.

45
Fw 190A-4 'Yellow 6' of Oberleutnant Hans Beisswenger, Staffelkapitän 6./JG 54, Ryelbitzi, February 1943
One last look at a typical winter finish already becoming stained and worn from hard use. A member of II. Gruppe since the autumn of 1940 (and Staffelkapitän of 6./JG 54 since 10 August 1942), a greater part of Beisswenger's 152 victories were achieved on the Bf 109. He flew the 190 for only a matter of weeks before being reported missing over Lake Ilmen on 6 March 1943.

46
Fw 190A-9 'Yellow 1' of Hauptmann Helmut Wettstein, Staffelkapitän 6./JG 54, Libau-Grobin/Courland, February 1945
After earlier serving as Staffelkapitän of 1./JG 54 (see profile 31), Wettstein ended the war in Courland at the head of 6. Staffel. His closely-dappled 'Anton-9' shown here is typical of the period with simplified national insignia. Helmut Wettstein had scored the 'Green Heart's' 8000th victory of the war over Courland on 15 October 1944. He ended the war with 43 kills.

47
Fw 190A-8 'Yellow 1' of Leutnant Gerd Thyben, Staffelkapitän 7./JG 54, Libau-Grobin/Courland, circa January 1945
Another drab late war finish with simplified insignia, but enlivened in this instance by a tightly spiralled spinner. Thyben had come to II./JG 54 in April 1944 after first serving with JG 3 in Southern Russia. Heading 7.Staffel by the war's end, he had scored 152 Eastern Front victories (plus 5 in the west). His final victim on 8 May 1945 was also the very last of the nearly 9500 enemy aircraft claimed destroyed by the 'Green Hearts' in World War 2.

48
Fw 190A-4 'Yellow 2' of Oberfeldwebel Heinrich Sterr, 6./JG 54, circa March 1943
Indicative of the spring thaw period, II.Gruppe also removed large areas of winter white to reveal the two-tone green beneath. They sometimes added an extra refinement, however, by applying patches of black to break up the aircraft's outline even further. Sterr who, like Robert Weiss, rejoiced in the nickname 'Bazi' (a Bavarian and Austrian colloquialism for 'Rascal'), had joined II./JG 54 in 1942. He scored 127 kills in the east – most of them on Fw 190s – before transferring to IV.Gruppe and Defence of the Reich duties in late 1944. He was downed by a P-51 on 26 November 1944 while attempting to land at Vörden.

49
Fw 190A-8 'White 3' of Oberleutnant Karl Brill, Staffelkapitän 10./JG 54, Lemberg (Lwow)/-Poland, summer 1944
Newly equipped with A-8s in preparation for Defence of the Reich, IV./JG 54 suddenly found itself sent eastwards in the summer of 1944. 'White 3' is representative of the Gruppe's aircraft at that time. Mindful of JG 54's tradition, the Gruppe badge on the cowling is a stylised version of the Königsberg coat-of-arms on a 'Green Heart' background. The Navajo indian's head beneath the cockpit is the badge of 10.Staffel (subsequently redesignated 13./JG 54). Brill is credited with 35 kills, but it is unknown how many of these were gained in the east.

50
Fw 190F-2 'Black Chevron and Bars' of Major Alfred Druschel, Geschwaderkommodore, Schl.G 1, Varvarovka, Summer 1943
Kommodore of the first Fw 190-equipped Schlachtgeschwader, Druschel opted for pre-war fighter style command markings, rather than the more usual triple-chevron of a Schlacht-Kommodore on this remarkably clean-looking F-2. His operational career of some 800 combat missions encompassed Stalingrad, Kursk and the Crimea, but the exact number of his victories – certainly enough to qualify him for Eastern Front acedom – has never been established. After over a year in staff positions, he returned to operations in December 1944 as Kommodore of SG 4 in the west, only to disappear somewhere over the Ardennes on New Year's Day 1945, en route to attack Allied airfields as part of Operation Bodenplatte. He remains missing to this day.

51
Fw 190F-2 'Black Double Chevron' of Hauptmann Georg Dörffel, Gruppenkommandeur I/Schl.G 1, Kharkov, circa February 1943
Displaying a textbook set of early markings for the first-generation Fw 190 Schlachtgeschwader, Dörffel's F-2 combines the double chevron of a Gruppenkommandeur with the solid black triangle of the ground-attack arm. This latter dates back to the Hs 123 Gruppen of the late 1930s. Schl.G 1 initially used it to differentiate between Gruppen: I Gruppe machines carried the triangle forward of the fuselage cross on both sides of the fuselage (hence Dörffel's chevrons – and all individual letters – had to be displayed in the aft station); II.Gruppe positioned the triangle behind the cross on both sides. 'Orge' Dörffel scored 30 kills in the east. Later heading SG 4 in Italy, he was killed in action northwest of Rome on 26 May 1944.

52

Fw 190F-2 'Black Chevron' of Oberleutnant Karl Kennel, *Staffelkapitän* 5./Schl.G 1, Varvarovka, July 1943

Kennel's machine shows that Schl.G 1 had abandoned the solid black triangle prior to *Zitadelle* in favour of an amended fighter-style system: I.*Gruppe* devoid of markings behind the fuselage cross, II.*Gruppe* carrying a horizontal bar. Here the similarity ended, for each *Staffelkapitän* displayed a single black chevron, and *Staffel* members were identified by letter – and not by number – in the respective *Staffel* colours of white, black and green (note that, as with the fighters, all previous red markings had now been deleted to avoid confusion with the enemy's insignia). Kennel himself would survive the war with 34 victories, all but three scored on the Eastern Front.

53

Fw 190F-2 'White A' of Leutnant Fritz Seyffardt, 6./Schl.G 1, Ukraine, circa May 1943

Seyffardt's F-2 illustrates the white individual coding initially adopted by 6./Schl.G 1 upon their return to the Eastern Front after conversion from the Bf 109 to Fw 190, and prior to their being allocated green as their definitive *Staffel* colour. Subsequently serving with 5./SG 2, Seyffardt ended the war as *Staffelkapitän* of 12./SG 151 still flying ground-attack sorties against Soviet forces in Germany. His aerial victories totalled 30, many of them *Stormoviks*.

54

Fw 190F-2 'Black T' of Oberfeldwebel Otto Dommeratzky, 8./Schl.G 1, Southern Sector, September 1943

As a member of the semi-autonomous Fw 190 and Hs 129-equipped 8./Schl.G 1, Dommeratzky flew this heavily mottled and somewhat worse for wear F-2 in the Kiev area in the autumn of 1943. Later transferring to 6./SG 2, he had claimed some 38 aerial kills before himself being shot down by marauding US fighters over Czechoslovakia on 13 October 1944.

55

Fw 190D-9 'Black Chevron and Bars' of Oberst Hans-Ulrich Rudel, *Geschwaderkommodore* SG 2, Grossenhain, April 1945

The most highly decorated member of the entire *Wehrmacht* (and the sole recipient of the Golden Oak Leaves), Rudel's career flying the Ju 87 in Russia is legendary. His unit continued to employ anti-tank Ju 87s long after all other SGs had converted to the Fw 190. But in the closing weeks of the war he too was persuaded to fly the single-seater. Among several issued to *Stab* SG 2, the *Kommodore's* own D-9, seen here, shows evidence of overpainting before application of the command insignia which had previously adorned his Ju 87G. Having sunk a battleship, a cruiser, a destroyer and over 70 landing craft, and destroyed over 500 enemy tanks, 800 soft-skinned vehicles, 150 artillery positions, four armoured trains, and bridges too numerous to mention, Rudel's tally of nine aerial kills almost pales into insignificance!

56

Fw 190F-2 'Black Double Chevron' of Major Heinz Frank, *Gruppenkommandeur* II./SG 2, Karankut/Crimea, April 1944

A standard *Kommandeur's* double chevron forward of the fuselage cross and the horizontal bar aft identify this clean-looking F-2 as the mount of Heinz 'Allan' Frank, a long-time *Schlacht* pilot who had flown his first missions over Poland and France on the Hs 123. He died in hospital on 7 October 1944 after the accidental discharge of a pistol left a bullet in his hip. His score of aerial kills stood at eight.

57

Fw 190F-9 'Black Double Chevron/2' of Major Karl Kennel, *Gruppenkommandeur* II./SG 2, Börgönd/Hungary, circa December 1944

Having risen from *Staffelkapitän* of 5./Schl.G 1 to become *Kommandeur* of II./SG 2 for the final nine months of the war, Kennel's F-9 graphically illustrates the importance played by camouflage in the winter of 1944-45. The *Schlachtflieger* were now equally, if not more, at risk of being caught by marauding Allied fighters on the ground than they were when in the air. The significance of the darker nose ring is not known (it may simply have been a replacement), but the yellow wraparound chevron on both upper and lower surfaces of the port wing was the standard in-theatre recognition marking of all Hungarian-based low-flying attack aircraft, Fw 190 and Ju 87 alike.

58

Fw 190F-8 'Black Chevron' of Leutnant Hermann Buchner, *Staffelkapitän* 4./SG 2, Zilistea/Rumania, June 1944

Anoher well-used F-8, Buchner's 'White L' wears an indian's head badge superficially similar to that of 10./JG 54 (see profile 49), but was, in fact, purely a personal insignia applied to the aircraft during his time as *Kapitän* of 4./SG 2 in the summer of 1944. Previously a member of Bleckmann's highly successful 6.*Staffel*, Buchner had flown many escort missions for SG 2's *Stukas* and had scored 46 victories before transition to the Me 262 in the autumn of 1944. With III./JG 7 in Defence of the Reich he subsequently added 12 US heavy bombers to his tally.

59

Fw 190A-5 'Black G' of Oberfeldwebel August Lambert, 5./SG 2, Southern Sector, late 1943

A somewhat weathered and undistinguished aircraft for the most successful of them all. During the Crimean campaign of 1944 Lambert's score rocketed; in the three week battle of Sevastopol alone it went from 20 to 90! After a spell as an instructor, Lambert returned to operations in the closing weeks of the war as *Staffelkapitän* of 8./SG 77. His 'Black 9' was downed by P-51s near Dresden on 17 April 1945, his total standing at 116 – by far the highest of any *Schlachtflieger*.

60

Fw 190F-8 'Black Chevron/Green H' of

Hauptmann Günther Bleckmann, *Staffelkapitän* 6./SG 2, Bacau/Rumania, May 1944

Bleckmann's F-8 carries his *Kapitän*'s chevron applied ahead of the individual aircraft letter as per the book. Heading 6./SG 2 for over a year, Bleckmann also served at times as acting *Kommandeur* of II.*Gruppe*. Having flown numerous escort sorties for SG 2's remaining Ju 87s, Bleckmann's score had reached 27 when he was killed on 4 June 1944 in a crash south of Jasy, Rumania, after his aircraft caught fire in the air while returning from another such mission.

FIGURE PLATES

1

3./JG 54's Oberfeldwebel Otto Kittel, the top scoring Fw 190 pilot on the Eastern Front, is seen wearing his one-piece winter overalls, equipped with a fur collar, in the northern secto in early 1944. He is also wearing a standard issue fur cap. Note the diagonal line of the upper body zip on the suit.

2

The highest scoring *Schlachtflieger* of them all, Leutnant August Lambert of 5./SG 2 is wearing a two-piece black leather flying suit– a popular choice amongst many single-seat fighter and attack pilots throughout the war. He has his trousers tucked into standard issue flying boots, and a Walther PP pistol and compass adorn his waist belt. Note that Lambert has a simple silk scarf draped around his neck – this was replaced in the summer of 1944 by the Knight's Cross.

3

The long-time *Kommodore* of JG 54, Oberstleutnant Hannes Trautloft stood head and shoulders above most other pilots in the *Geschwader* due to his loft frame (6 ft 4 in) and bear-like build. he is seen here in the autumn of 1943 wearing his favourite leather jacket, with fur collar, officers' breesches and knee-length flying boots. Trautloft's Knight's Cross and rank tabs are just visible beneath his jacket.

4

Compared to the stylish leather suits and jackets worn in the winter months on the Russian Front, Oberfeldwebel Hermann Buchner of 4./SG 2 models the simple lightweight summer tunic and breeches so favoured by the lower flying ranks in the warm summer months. On his sleeve are Oberfeldwebel's 'moustaches' – flying overall rank badges – and he is wearing a 1943 pattern cap. Buchner flew over 600 missions in the east, and finished the war an ace.

5

Without a doubt the most famous Fw 190 pilot of them all, Walter Nowotny (here, an Oberleutnant) was a fighting legend within the Luftwaffe. The first man past the magical 250 kills mark, he is seen here at around the time this milestone was passed in October 1943. He is wearing a lightweight summer shirt with the sleeves rolled down, a full Fallschirm30/1 parachute and harness and his famous 'victory trousers', patched up with leather at the knees. These were worn on every mission following Nowotny's dunking in the Baltic in July 1941. Salt-stained and torn by barbed wire, the breeches are tucked into far newer flying boots. On his head he wears a Netzkopfhaube lightweight flying helmet, and above his Knight's Cross with Oak Leaves and Swords is a standard issue throat mike, popular amongst Fw 190 pilots in-theatre. Trailing over his back is the lead for the mike.

6

Oberleutnant Joachim Brendel, a 189-victory ace with JG 51, wears similar rig to Nowotny, although his breeches are genuine 'baggy' flight trousers with deep knee pockets. Again he is also wearing a 1943 issue soft cap. Unlike the other five pilots featured in these plates, Brendel is wearing lace up shoes, as well as a black tie behind his Knight's cross. This was how he appeared in the spring of 1944.

Fw 190 Eastern Front Orders of Battle 1943-45

(A) 10 July 1943 (Battle of Kursk)

Luftflotte 1 (Leningrad area)

	Strength	Serviceable
Stab JG 54	5	5
II./JG 54 (Fw190/Bf 109)	50	28
12./JG 54	11	8

Luftflotte 6 (Kursk Northern Flank)

	Strength	Serviceable
Stab JG 51	15	10
I./JG 51	28	15
III./JG 51	35	19
IV./JG 51	30	25
[15.(span.)/JG 51	22	16]
I./JG 54	32	19

Luftflotte 4 (Kursk Southern Flank)

	Strength	Serviceable
Stab Schl.G 1	2	1
I./Schl.G 1 (Fw 190/Hs 129)	51	36
II./Schl.G 1 (Fw 190/Hs 129)	54	38

TOTALS:	**335**	**220**

(B) 26 June 1944 (Soviet Summer Offensive)

Luftflotte 1 (Northern Sector)
Gefechtsverband Kuhlmey (Finland)

		Strength		Serviceable
II./JG 54	Immola	28		19
1./JG 54	Turku	12		9
1./SG 5	Immola	12		5

Jagdabschnittsführer Ostland (Estonia)

Stab JG 54	Dorpat	12		7
I./JG 54 [minus 1.]				
	Reval-Laksberg	22		13

Luftflotte 6 (Central Sector)
1. Fliegerdivision

Stab SG1	Pastovichi	5	-	4
III./SG 1	Pastovichi	38	-	20
I./SG 10	Bobruisk	36		22

4. Fliegerdivision

III./SG 10	Dokudovo	39	30

Jagdabschnittsführer 6
Stabsstaffel JG 51

(Fw 190/Bf109)	Orscha	12	11

Luftflotte 4 (Southern Sector)
I. Fliegerkorps (Rumania)

II./SG 2	Zilistea	27	20
II./SG 10	Culm	29	18

VIII. Fliegerkorps (Poland)

II./SG 77	Lemberg (Lvov)	33	24

TOTALS:	**305**	**202**

(C) 1 April 1945 (Post-Bodenplatte build-up)

Luftflotte 1 (North)
Luftwaffenkommando Courland

Stab JG 54	5	4
I./JG 54	38	33
II./JG 54	40	37
III./SG 3	43	42

Luftwaffenkommando Ostpreussen

Stab(Staffel) JG 51	22	21
I./SG 3	45	31

Luftflotte 6 (Centre)

Stab JG 1	4	4
II./JG 1	68	67
Stab JG 3	5	5
[II./JG 3]		
IV./JG 3	58	47
II./JG 4	57	57
Stab JG 6 (Fw 190/Bf 109)	4	4
I./JG 6	72	55
II./JG 6	47	45
Stab JG 11	4	4
I./JG 11	45	45
III./JG 11	45	44
III./JG 54	42	42
[II./JG 300]		
[II./JG 301]		
[III./JG 301]		
Stab SG 1	3	3
I./SG 1	42	38
II./SG 1	44	39
III./SG 1 (minus 8.)	41	20
Stab SG 2	6	6
II./SG 2	49	49
Stab SG 3	8	7
II./SG 3	43	40
Stab SG4	1	1
I./SG 4	29	19
II./SG 4	39	32
III./SG 4	21	9
1.(Pz)/SG 9	16	15
Stab SG 77	8	7
I./SG 77	34	33
II./SG 77	35	29
III./SG 77	45	41
13./SG 151	18	18

Luftflotte 4 (South)

I./SG 2	28	19
Stab SG 10	6	4
I./SG 10	19	9
II./SG 10	4	0
III./SG 10	33	17
ung.Schl.Gr. (Hungarian)	23	12

TOTALS:	**1239**	**1054**